TOFU
Cookery

by Louise Hagler

Revised Edition

The Book Publishing Company • Summertown, Tennessee 38483

Other books by Louise Hagler

Tofu Quick and Easy

Great new time-saving menu tips that emphasize tofu's versatility in over 120 delicious dishes.
96 pages $8.95

Lighten Up!

Tasty, Low-Fat, Low-Calorie Vegetarian Cuisine

Trim fat, cut calories, add fiber, and eliminate cholesterol from your diet. Over 130 easy-to-prepare recipes open the way to full-flavored taste treats that will delight and satisfy!
160 pages $11.95

Soyfoods Cookery

Discover the delicious diversity of soyfoods. Learn easy ways to add the healthful benefits of soy to your diet.
112 pages $9.95

All books include nutritional analyses for all recipes.

Ask your store to carry these books, or you may order directly from:

The Book Publishing Company
P.O. Box 99
Summertown, TN 38483

or call: 1-800-695-2241
Please add $2.50 per book for shipping

Editor: **Louise Hagler**
Recipe Testing Coordinator: **Colleen Pride**
Food Stylists: **Jane Ayers, Louise Hagler**
Photographers: **Michael Bonnickson, Thomas Johns**

Managing Editors: **Jane Ayers, Cynthia Holzapfel**
Nutritional Consultant: **Margaret Nofziger**
Art: **Peter Hoyt, Gregory Lowry**
Soyfoods Consultants: **Laurie Praskin, Suzy Jenkins-Viavant**

Cover Photo: Enchiladas (page 66); Honey Cheesecake with Kiwis and Blueberries (page 139); and Almond Salad (page 28).

ISBN 0-913990-76-0

Hagler, Louise
    Tofu Cookery / by Louise Hagler. — Rev. ed.
       p. cm.
    Includes index.
    ISBN 0-913990-76-0 : $15.95
    1. Cookery (Tofu) I. Title
TX814 . 5 . T63H338 1990
641.6'5655—dc20   90-20943
                                                        CIP

4 5 7 6 8 9 0   99 98 97

Copyright 1982, 1991 The Book Publishing Company, Summertown, Tennessee 38483

Acknowledgments
Our special thanks go to the following people from The Farm in Summertown, Tennessee, for originating and developing the recipes in this book: Dorothy Bates, Stewart Butler, Beth Cramer, Mary Felber, Claire Fitch, Louise Hagler, Nancy Haren, Sarah Hergenrather, Dawn Huddleston, Jane Hunnicutt, Sylvia Hupp, Suzy Jenkins-Viavant, Roberta Kachinsky, Betsy Keller, Marion Lyon, Kathryn McClure, Earlynn McIntyre, Cornelia Mandelstein, Lee Meltzer, Ann Moore, Stacey Moore, Laurie Praskin, Carol Pratt, Colleen Pride, Rachel Scythe, Honey Tepper, Ruth Thomas, Lani Young.

Thanks to James Egan, Eleanor Dale Evans, Leon Fainbuch, Ellen Isaacs, and John Pielaszczyk for layout and typography.

Table of Contents

Introducing Tofu

Today, tofu hardly needs an introduction. It has truly become a household word. Many have paid tribute to this noble soy food. Although it has been the brunt of several jokes on TV sitcoms, that only shows the extent of its entry into the national culture. The fact still remains: tofu is one of the most versatile protein foods in the world. For the few who still may not have been introduced, tofu, also know as "bean curd," is made by curding the mild white "milk" of the soybean. It is high in protein and relatively low in calories, fats, and carbohydrates. Tofu is an economical source of protein and contains no cholesterol.

Tofu originated in Asia over 2,000 years ago where it still takes many and varied forms not generally seen or available in this country. The recipes in this book try to incorporate the use of tofu in ways that are recognizable to the western palate. These are only a sampling of the culinary delights possible with tofu, ranging from the familiar to the international and exotic. Tofu can be prepared in a variety of main dishes, breads, desserts, soups, salads, salad dressings, and dips for any meal, snack or party.

In this revised edition, I have tried to bring the recipes up to date for today's nutritional standards. I have also added new recipes that reflect more healthful, quick and easy cooking. Overall, the fat and salt contents of the recipes have been greatly reduced and the frying of foods has been eliminated wherever possible.

With its growing popularity, tofu has become easy to find in supermarkets everywhere, usually in the produce section along with oriental vegetables. It can also be found in many oriental food shops and natural or health food stores. Tofu shops and plants have been sprouting up around the country. If you become a serious tofu chef or use large amounts of tofu, you might want to make arrangements to get it right from the source; or you can make your own tofu at home (see directions on page 155).

Tofu is also an excellent food for babies, children, and the elderly because it is a wholesome, complete vegetable protein that is very easy to digest. It is a good food for sensitive stomachs. For babies, tofu can be blended in the blender or ground in a baby food grinder with whatever flavoring, fruit, or vegetable you like.

Each recipe has a nutritional analysis, giving the amount per serving of calories, protein, fat, and carbohydrates. These are intended only as a guideline for those concerned with these figures. The analyses don't include any fat used for frying, unless the amount is specified in the recipe, or oil and flour used in pan preparation for baking; neither do they include optional ingredients or anything listed as a serving suggestion. The "Per Serving" calculations are figured on the average number of servings listed with the recipe. If two options for an ingredient are listed, the first one is used.

The nutritional content of tofu will vary slightly depending on what strain of bean was used and what method was used to process it. The statistics used to calculate the nutritional analyses in this book came from the USDA.

120 grams of tofu	
(approx. ¼ lb. or ½ cup)	
Calories	86.0
Protein	9.4 gm
Fat	5.0 gm
Carbohydrates	2.9 gm
Calcium	154.0 mg
Iron	2.0 mg
Sodium	8.0 mg
Potassium	50.0 mg
Niacin	trace
Riboflavin	trace
Thiamin	trace

As you gain experience using tofu, you can adapt many of your own favorite recipes to include it. Tofu fits easily as a low calorie dressing, whip, or dip; as an inexpensive alternative to meat, fish, poultry, or cheese; or as a protein extender in baked goods. There is a whole new world of cooking and eating awaiting you using this nutritious, multifaceted food from the East. Happy cooking and eating!

Louise Hagler
1990

Spaghetti Primavera, page 46

GETTING TO KNOW YOUR TOFU

Buying and Handling Tofu

Tofu can be made or bought in several different forms. These range from silken tofu, which is the softest form, to a medium soft Japanese-style, to a medium firm Chinese-style, to hard pressed tofu, which is a very dense and firm cheese. There are many forms available in between, depending on how the tofu was made.

Fresh tofu has a fresh and delicate scent to it. This is tofu at its best. It barely has any smell at all when really fresh. Each package of tofu should show an expiration date. Be sure to check for this when buying tofu.

If fresh tofu is handled right, it can keep for up to one week in your refrigerator. It should be kept submerged in cold water, and the water should be changed daily to keep it fresh and moist.

The firmer types of tofu are best used for slicing or cubing and sometimes crumbling. The softer tofu can be used for slicing and cubing, also, but it does not hold its shape well if it is handled a lot. The softer kinds of tofu are best for blending, mashing, and crumbling.

If you want a firm tofu and you can only find soft, you can slice the tofu into slabs, place the slabs side by side between towels, and set another towel and a heavy breadboard or other similar weight on it for 20 to 30 minutes.

If the tofu you buy smells a little sour, it is still usable, but it is best to boil it for about twenty minutes, which will change its texture somewhat, making it hard and chewier. We do not recommend

Tofu Blocks

using tofu in this state for blending in a blender or for use in any dessert or fresh salad or dip. If the tofu you buy smells very sour, we suggest that you return it to your grocer for a replacement and recommend that he keep it at a cooler temperature.

Measuring Tofu

There are a couple of ways to measure tofu when it is not pre-measured for you in a package. If you are going to slice or cube the tofu, use the water displacement method. Fill a 4-cup measuring cup with 3 cups water. Then float a block of tofu that brings the water level up to the 4-cup level. This will give you ½ lb. of tofu.

You may have to take a slice off the block if the water level rises above the 4-cup mark. If the water doesn't reach the 4-cup level when you put the block in, add a slice or two until the water level comes up to 4 cups. Be sure to check at eye level when measuring, and don't press the tofu down under the water. If you are going to blend, mash, or crumble the tofu, you can measure it in a measuring cup in the mashed or crumbled form. One cup is equal to ½ lb. of tofu.

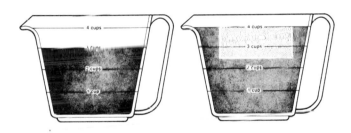

Displacement Method of Measuring Tofu

Blending Tofu

When you are blending tofu, there are a few points to remember. Blend it as you would any dense material and don't try to do too much at a time. In a standard home blender, it is a good rule to blend no more than ½ lb. at a time, but this could vary with different types of blenders and the softness of the tofu. It will help to mash or crumble your tofu before blending if it is not very soft.

Unless the tofu is quite soft, you will not be able to put everything in the blender, turn it on and leave it to blend. It will probably need to be coaxed from the sides gently with a rubber spatula to keep it circulating. Be careful not to touch the blades with the spatula. If you don't have a blender, an electric mixer works well on the softer tofu. A food processor will also work, but generally does not make as creamy a finished product as a blender.

If a recipe calls for more than ½ lb. of tofu to be blended in a blender along with other ingredients, you can break up the tofu in a bowl and add the other ingredients. Then, stir it all up and divide the mixture into smaller batches to blend. Use only about ½ lb. of tofu per batch. Then, put it all together again in a bowl and stir well.

Frozen Tofu

Freezing tofu drastically changes its properties, and transforms it into a unique protein food. When you freeze it, thaw it, and squeeze out the water, the tofu resembles a spongy latticework, which has a more meaty, chewy consistency than regular tofu. It soaks up marinades and sauces more readily than the plain form. To freeze tofu, just drain it, wrap it in foil or plastic, and put it in the freezer until frozen into a solid block. You can let it thaw at room temperature, in the microwave, or pour boiling water over it as needed. Frozen tofu adds yet more variety to an already versatile food.

Marinating

Tofu and marinades were meant for each other. Always marinate in glass, stainless steel, or enamel. Marinating slices or cubes of tofu works best in a flat pan. See Korean Barbeque, p. 81. The pieces should be carefully turned several times, or you can use a turkey baster to suck the marinade up and squirt it back over the pieces. With frozen tofu, you will need to mix and squeeze the marinade into the tofu. When a recipe calls for marinating tofu for one hour or less, it can be done at room temperature covered with wax paper or a towel. For longer periods of time, marinating should be done in a tightly covered container in the refrigerator because of the risk of bacterial growth.

Dips and Spreads

Clockwise from top left: Pimento Dip or Spread, Walnut Olive Dip, and Parsley-Onion Dip

DIPS AND SPREADS

A medium soft tofu or Japanese-style tofu is the best for dips. Dips are creamiest when made in a blender, but can also be made with a food processor or electric mixer. Read "Blending Tofu" on p. 7. Use very fresh tofu for making dips. For lower calorie dips and spreads, you can leave out the oil. Most dips taste best if you make them ahead of time and let them sit in the refrigerator for several hours to fully develop the flavors.

Dry Onion Soup Dip

Makes 2¾ cups

This is the classic California dip made with tofu.

Blend in a food processor or blender until smooth and creamy:
> **1 lb. soft tofu**
> **2 Tbsp. oil**
> **2 Tbsp. fresh lemon juice**
> **1 Tbsp. sweetener of your choice**

Stir or blend in:
> **1 pkg. (scant ½ cup) dry onion soup
> mix**

This is best if refrigerated for about 4 hours to overnight to let the flavors blend.

Per ¼ Cup Serving: Calories: 68, Protein: 4 gm., Fat: 5 gm., Carbohydrates: 4 gm.

Variation: If you'd rather not use a package mix to flavor this dip, replace it with:
> **⅓ cup dried, minced onions**
> **1 Tbsp. vegetable bouillon granules**
> **1 tsp. garlic powder**

Per ¼ Cup Serving: Calories: 89, Protein: 3 gm., Fat: 7 gm., Carbohydrates: 3 gm.

Walnut-Olive Dip

Makes 1¾ cups

Blend in a food processor or blender until smooth and creamy:

½ lb. soft tofu
3 Tbsp. fresh lemon juice
1 Tbsp. oil

2 tsp. sweetener of your choice
½ tsp. salt

Fold in:

2 Tbsp. walnuts, finely chopped
4 tsp. black olives, chopped

Per ¼ Cup Serving: Calories: 73, Protein: 3 gm., Fat: 4 gm., Carbohydrates: 3 gm.

Chive Dip

Makes 2½ cups

Blend in a food processor or blender until smooth and creamy:

1 lb. soft tofu
2 Tbsp. oil
1 Tbsp. vinegar

1 Tbsp. soy sauce
½ tsp. garlic powder
¼ tsp. black pepper

Fold in:

¼ cup fresh chives, chopped

Per ¼ Cup Serving: Calories: 63, Protein: 4 gm., Fat: 5 gm., Carbohydrates: 2 gm.

Dill Dip

Makes 1¼ cups

Blend in a food processor or blender until smooth and creamy:

¾ cup soft tofu
2½ Tbsp. wine vinegar
1 Tbsp. oil
1 Tbsp. onion, minced
1½ tsp. sweetener of your choice

1 tsp. salt
1 tsp. dill weed
 or 1 Tbsp. fresh dill
⅛ tsp. black pepper

Per ¼ Cup Serving: Calories: 56, Protein: 3 gm, Fat: 4 gm., Carbohydrates: 2 gm.

Almond Dip

Makes 1½ cups

Blend in a food processor or blender until smooth and creamy:
- ½ lb. soft tofu
- 3 Tbsp. fresh lemon juice
- 1 Tbsp. oil
- 2 tsp. sweetener of your choice
- ½ tsp. salt

Fold in:
- ¼ cup roasted slivered almonds

Per ¼ Cup Serving: Calories: 91, Protein: 5 gm., Fat: 6 gm., Carbohydrates: 5 gm.

Pimento Dip or Spread

Makes 2 cups

Good for sandwich filling, on crackers, or as a dip.

Blend in a food processor or blender until smooth and creamy:
- ½ cup soft tofu
- 2 Tbsp. oil
- 2 Tbsp. apple cider vinegar
- 1 Tbsp. sweetener of your choice
- 1 tsp. salt
- ⅛ tsp. black pepper
- pinch of garlic powder

Fold in:
- ¾ lb. tofu, crumbled
- 3 Tbsp. sweet pickle relish
- ½ cup pimentos, chopped

This is best if refrigerated overnight.

Per ¼ Cup Serving: Calories: 87, Protein: 5 gm., Fat: 6 gm., Carbohydrates: 5 gm.

Miso-Ginger Dip

Makes about 1¼ cups

Chop in a food processor or blender:
- 1½" cube fresh ginger root (this can be more or less to taste)
- 1 clove fresh garlic
- 1" cube fresh onion

Add to the food processor and blend all together:
- ½ lb. tofu
- 2 Tbsp. white miso
- 1½ Tbsp. fresh lemon juice

Serve with crackers or raw vegetables.

Per ¼ Cup Serving: Calories: 53, Protein: 4 gm., Fat: 2 gm., Carbohydrates: 5 gm.

Curry Paste Dip

Good with raw vegetables.

Blend in a food processor or blender until smooth and creamy:
½ lb. soft tofu
3 Tbsp. curry paste (commercially prepared)
2 Tbsp. fresh lemon juice

Fold in:
1 cup chopped cucumber

Per ¼ Cup Serving: Calories: 35, Protein: 3 gm., Fat: 1 gm., Carbohydrates: 3 gm.

Caper Spread

Blend in a food processor or blender until smooth and creamy:
½ lb. soft tofu   **1 tsp. dijon mustard**
2 Tbsp. caper juice   **½ tsp. salt**
1 Tbsp. oil

Pour this into a bowl which has been rubbed with:
1 clove garlic, cut in half

Fold in:
1 Tbsp. onion, finely minced
1 Tbsp. capers (large ones, cut in half)

Per ¼ Cup Serving: Calories: 49, Protein: 3 gm., Fat: 4 gm., Carbohydrates: 1 gm.

Cilantro-Jalapeno Dip

Serve with blue or yellow corn chips.

Chop in a food processor or blender:
1 cup loosely packed fresh cilantro   **1 clove garlic**
leaves   **1 small jalapeno***

Add to the processor and blend until smooth and creamy:
½ lb. soft tofu   **1 Tbsp. fresh lime or lemon juice**
1 Tbsp. oil   **½ tsp. salt**

*Add jalapeno with care, as peppers vary in "heat." You might want to start with half a pepper and taste the dip. Add more to taste.

Per ¼ Cup Serving: Calories: 59, Protein: 4 gm., Fat: 5 gm., Carbohydrates: 1 gm.

Guacamole Dip

Makes 2 cups

Mash:
  2 ripe avocados (about 1½ cups)

Stir in:
  ¾ cup tomato, chopped
  ½ cup Tofu Salad Dressing, p. 42
  ½ cup green taco sauce
  2 tsp. onion powder
  or ¼ cup finely chopped onion

  1 tsp. garlic powder
  or 3 cloves garlic, pressed
  ½ tsp. salt

Per ¼ Cup Serving: Calories: 111, Protein: 2 gm., Fat: 4 gm., Carbohydrates: 7 gm.

Jalapeno Dip

Makes 1¾ cups

This dip is for folks who like it "hot"!

Blend in a food processor or blender until smooth and creamy:
  ¾ lb. soft tofu
  2 Tbsp. oil
  1 pickled jalapeno pepper,
  more or less to taste

  ½ small onion, chopped
  2 Tbsp. fresh parsley
  ½ tsp. salt

Chill for two hours before serving.

This dip is hot by American standards, and gets hotter after it has been chilled.

Per ¼ Cup Serving: Calories: 74, Protein: 4 gm., Fat: 6 gm., Carbohydrates: 2 gm.

Garlic Dip

Makes 2¾ cups

Chop in a food processor or blender:
  4 cloves garlic

Add and process until smooth and creamy:
  ½ lb. soft tofu
  2 Tbsp. oil
  2 Tbsp. fresh lemon juice

  1 Tbsp. sweetener of your choice
  ½ tsp. salt

Per ¼ Cup Serving: Calories: 78, Protein: 3 gm., Fat: 6 gm., Carbohydrates: 3 gm.

Parsley-Onion Dip

Blend in a food processor or blender until smooth and creamy:
1 lb. soft tofu
½ cup fresh parsley leaves
1 small red onion, chopped (1/3 cup)
  or 2 tsp. onion powder
2 Tbsp. oil
2 Tbsp. fresh lemon juice
1 tsp. salt

Per ¼ Cup Serving: Calories: 56, Protein: 3 gm., Fat: 4 gm., Carbohydrates: 2 gm.

Green Onion Dip

A light green colored dip with a green onion nip.

Chop in a food processor or blender:
½ cup green onion, cup up
½ cup fresh parsley leaves, loosely packed

Add and process until smooth and creamy:
½ lb. tofu
1 Tbsp. fresh lemon juice
1 Tbsp. oil
¼ tsp. salt

Per ¼ Cup Serving: Calories: 66, Protein: 4 gm., Fat: 5 gm., Carbohydrates: 3 gm.

Soups

Zucchini Bisque and Basic Fried Tofu sandwich

SOUPS

Zucchini Bisque

Makes 6 cups

Saute:
- **2 Tbsp. olive oil**
- **1 medium onion, chopped**
- **1½ lbs. zucchini, sliced**

Add to the sauteed vegetables, cover and simmer 20 minutes:
- **2½ cups stock or water**
- **½ tsp. nutmeg**
- **1/8 tsp. freshly ground black pepper**

Remove from heat and let cool 5 minutes.

Blend in a blender until smooth and creamy:
- **½ lb. tofu**
- **1 Tbsp. olive oil**

Stir blended tofu mixture into sauteed vegetables. Heat, but do not boil. Add salt to taste.

Per 1 Cup Serving: Calories: 119, Protein: 5 gm., Fat: 8 gm., Carbohydrates: 8 gm.

Mushroom-Tofu Noodle Soup

Makes 3 quarts

Saute together in a soup pot:
- **2 Tbsp. olive oil**
- **1 medium onion, chopped**
- **1 cup carrot, sliced thinly**
- **1 cup celery, chopped**
- **¾ cup green pepper, chopped**
- **2 cloves garlic, minced**
- **6 oz. mushrooms, sliced**
- **1 lb. frozen tofu, thawed, squeezed dry and chopped small**

Add to the pot:
- **8 cups water**
- **6 cubes vegetable bouillon or 6 tsp. bouillon powder**

Bring to a boil and add:
- **6-8 oz. flat noodles**

Boil about 10 minutes or until noodles are al-dente. Serve

Per 1 Cup Serving: Calories: 113, Protein: 5 gm., Fat: 4 gm., Carbohydrates: 13 gm.

Minestrone Soup

Makes 11 cups

Freeze, thaw, squeeze out, and cut into ¾" cubes:
1 lb. tofu

Preheat oven to 375° F.

Mix together:
3 Tbsp. soy sauce
½ tsp. garlic powder

Mix and squeeze this mixture into tofu cubes. Then bake the cubes on an oiled cookie sheet for 10 minutes. Turn the cubes and bake 5 minutes more. Set aside.

Saute together for about 10 minutes:
2 Tbsp. olive oil
1 medium onion, chopped
2 carrots, sliced
1 medium zucchini, sliced

Combine the sauteed vegetables in a soup pot with:
1 (28 oz.) can tomatoes, chopped
4 cups water
2 cups tomato juice
2 tsp. basil
1 tsp. oregano
½ tsp. garlic powder
½ tsp. salt
¼ tsp. pepper

Bring to a boil and add:
3 oz. noodles or broken spaghetti

Simmer for 15 minutes, then add:
1 (15 oz.) can kidney beans
the browned tofu cubes

Serve when beans and tofu are heated through.

Per 1 Cup Serving: Calories: 167, Protein: 8 gm., Fat: 7 gm., Carbohydrates: 19 gm.

Curried Tofu-Apple Soup

Makes 3 quarts

A mild curried soup.

Freeze, thaw, squeeze dry, and cut or tear into bite-size pieces:
1½ lbs. tofu

Wash, pare, and dice:
4-5 apples

Heat to boiling:
2 qts. stock or water

Add apples and boil 2 minutes, then set aside, reserving liquid.

In another pan, saute together:
¼ cup oil
½ cup onions, chopped

When onions are almost transparent, add tofu and lightly fry.

While they are frying, sprinkle with:
⅓ cup unbleached white flour   **2 tsp. salt**
2 Tbsp. curry powder

Stir well, then add:
the cooked apples
2 cups water from the apple cooking pot

Stir constantly to avoid making lumps. Then pour it back into the apple cooking pot, stir, cover, and simmer 10-15 minutes. Serve

Per 1 Cup Serving: Calories: 139, Protein: 5 gm., Fat: 9 gm., Carbohydrates: 10 gm.

Tofu Chowder

Makes 2 quarts

Saute together for 15 minutes in a 4-6 quart pot:
2 Tbsp. oil   **2 carrots, chopped**
1 medium onion, chopped   **3 celery stalks, chopped**

Pour in:
2 cups water
2 cups soymilk

Add:
½ lb. tofu, crumbled   **½ tsp. black pepper**
2 tsp. salt   **½ tsp. celery seed**

Bring to a boil and add:
2 large potatoes, peeled and cubed (about 2 cups)

Simmer until potatoes are soft. Serve.

Per 1 Cup Serving: Calories: 130, Protein: 6 gm., Fat: 7 gm., Carbohydrates: 13 gm.

Tomato-Rice-Tofu Soup

Makes 5 cups

Saute together until soft:
1 Tbsp. olive oil
⅔ cup green pepper, chopped
⅔ cup onion, chopped
1 clove garlic, minced

Blend in a blender until smooth:
1 (16 oz.) can plum tomatoes and juice
or 1 lb. fresh tomatoes
1 can or 2 cups water

Pour blended tomatoes into the sauteed vegetables along with:

1 cup brown rice, cooked   **½ tsp. salt**
¼ lb. firm tofu, cut in small cubes   **¼ tsp. black pepper**
1 Tbsp. fresh parsley, chopped   **¼ tsp. allspice**
1 Tbsp. fresh basil, chopped

Stir and heat through, then serve.

Per 1 Cup Serving: Calories: 107, Protein: 4 gm., Fat: 4 gm., Carbohydrates: 15 gm.

Lentil Soup

Serves 6

Wash and drain:
1 cup lentils

Bring to a boil in a large pot with:
1 qt. water
½ tsp. salt

In a skillet, saute together:

2 Tbsp. oil   **1 medium carrot, sliced**
1 medium onion, diced   **1 celery stalk, sliced**
1 clove garlic, minced

When onion is soft, add all to boiling lentils with:
1 cup peeled tomatoes or
½ (6 oz.) can tomato paste

Simmer for another 30 minutes.

Add:

½ lb. tofu, cut in small cubes   **¼ tsp. basil**
1½ tsp. wine vinegar   **⅛ tsp. black pepper**

Continue simmering until lentils are soft. Serve.

Per 1 Cup Serving: Calories: 195, Protein: 12 gm., Fat: 6 gm., Carbohydrates: 25 gm.

Watercress or Bok Choy Soup

Makes 2½ quarts

A delicately flavored soup.

Dissolve in a soup pot:
2 quarts boiling water
4 cubes vegetable bouillon

Add:
½ lb. tofu, cut in 1½" x ¼" x ¼" pieces
1 small onion, diced or sliced in rounds

Simmer 10 to 15 minutes, then add:
1 bunch watercress, coarsely chopped

Cook 3 more minutes, then serve immediately.

Variation: Add about 25 Won Ton (see p. 93) in the last 5 minutes of cooking or 4 oz. flat noodles along with onion and tofu.

Variation: For Bok Choy Soup, chop ½ lb. bok choy diagonally every ½" and separate into stem and leaf pieces. Add stem pieces 4-5 minutes before serving. Add leaf pieces 3 minutes before serving.

Per 1 Cup Serving: Calories: 22, Protein: 2 gm., Fat: 1 gm., Carbohydrates: 2 gm.

Miso Soup

Serves 6

Miso is a salty, cultured bean paste from which soy sauce evolved. It can be found in the oriental food section of a supermarket or in a health food store.

Saute together in a soup pot until limp but not brown:
¼ cup oil   **4-6 carrots, sliced**
1 small head cabbage, shredded   **3 stalks celery, sliced**
3-4 small onions, diced

Add:
2 qts. hot water   **¼ tsp. black pepper**
1 tsp. salt

Simmer 30 minutes.

Cut into ¾" cubes and add to the soup:
1 lb. tofu

Dissolve together:
½ cup cold water
¼ cup miso

Stir into soup. Heat, but do not boil. Serve when tofu is heated through.

Per 1 Cup Serving: Calories: 98, Protein: 5 gm., Fat: 6 gm., Carbohydrates: 7 gm.

Watercress Soup with Won Ton

Hot and Sour Soup

Makes 6 cups

Bring to a boil:
4 cups water

Add:
½ lb. tofu, slivered
2 cups cabbage, thinly sliced
2 vegetable bouillon cubes

¾ tsp. salt
1 Tbsp. soy sauce

Simmer together for 3 minutes.

Add:
2 Tbsp. white vinegar
¼ tsp. cayenne

Bring back to a boil.

Dissolve together:
3 Tbsp. water
2 Tbsp. cornstarch

Stir the dissolved mixture into the soup. Serve garnished with chopped green onions and 2 tsp. Chinese sesame seed oil (optional).

Per 1 Cup Serving: Calories: 51, Protein: 4 gm., Fat: 2 gm., Carbohydrates: 5 gm.

Spring Soup

Makes 6 cups

Saute until crisp tender:
2 Tbsp. olive oil
1 cup scallions, chopped
1 carrot, in thin diagonal slices
1 stalk celery, in thin diagonal slices
2 cloves garlic, minced
¼ cup parsley, chopped

Stir in:
½ lb. frozen tofu, thawed, squeezed dry, and cut into bite-size pieces
4 cups water

Bring to a boil and add:
1 cup green peas
1 cup fresh spinach or watercress, chopped
1 bay leaf

When peas are tender, remove bay leaf and serve.

Per 1 Cup Serving: Calories: 116, Protein: 5 gm., Fat: 6 gm., Carbohydrates: 11 gm.

Mexican Corn Soup

This is a thick and hearty, savory soup.

Saute together until soft in a soup pot:
  2 Tbsp. olive oil
  1 cup onion, chopped
  ¾ cup green pepper, chopped
  3 cloves garlic, minced

Add to the pot:
  1 (15 oz.) can chopped tomatoes
  1 (30 oz.) can hominy, drained
  1 cup green peas, fresh or frozen
  ½ lb. frozen tofu, thawed, squeezed dry and cut into small pieces
  4 cups water
  1 tsp. cumin powder
  1 tsp. oregano
  ¼ cup fresh cilantro, chopped fine
  ½ medium jalapeno, sliced thin (more or less to taste)

Heat until boiling, and serve garnished with avocado slices and thin strips of corn tortilla on top.

Per 1 Cup Serving: Calories: 121, Protein: 5 gm., Fat: 3 gm., Carbohydrates: 20 gm.

Greek Salad

Salads

SALADS

Greek Salad

Serves 10-12

Pictured on page 27.

Dressing

Mix together:
  ¼ **cup olive oil**
  2 Tbsp. wine vinegar
  1 tsp. salt

  1 tsp. basil
  ½ **tsp. black pepper**
  ½ **tsp. oregano**

Pour the dressing over:
  1 lb. tofu, cut in ¾″ cubes

Marinate for at least 1 hour, stirring occasionally.

Wash, core and cut into wedges:
  3 fresh tomatoes

Wash and slice thin:
  3 cucumbers

Add these to the marinated tofu along with:
  ½ **large red onion, chopped**

  ½ **cup Greek or black olives**

Toss and serve on:
  1 head leaf lettuce, washed and dried

Per Serving: Calories: 111, Protein: 4 gm., Fat: 3 gm., Carbohydrates: 6 gm.

Almond Salad

Serves 6-8
Makes 4 cups

Combine in a bowl:
  1½ lbs. tofu, cut in ½″ cubes
  3 Tbsp. fresh lemon juice

  ½ **tsp. celery salt**

Mix in:
  1½ cups celery, diced
  ⅓ **cup green onion, minced**

  ¾ **cup almonds, slivered and toasted**
  ½ **tsp. salt**

Blend together with:
  1½ cups Tofu Sour Creme Dressing, p. 41

Chill and serve.

Per Serving: Calories: 267, Protein: 15 gm., Fat: 14 gm., Carbohydrates: 10 gm.

Spanish Tofu-Rice Salad

Marinate for ½ hour:

½ lb. tofu, cut in small cubes
1 tsp. salt

¼ cup lemon juice
¼ tsp. garlic powder

Mix together:

4 cups cooked rice
3 green onions, chopped
2 Tbsp. olive oil
1 green pepper, diced

¼ cup lemon juice
2 tomatoes, diced
3 tsp. salt

Mix this together with marinated tofu. Chill for a few hours.

Mix in:

¼-½ cup parsely, chopped

⅛ tsp. freshly ground black pepper

Serve.

Per Serving: Calories: 202, Protein: 5 gm., Fat: 5 gm., Carbohydrates: 33 gm.

Oriental Slaw

Chop in a blender or food processor:

1 clove garlic
1" cube fresh ginger root, peeled
¼ cup fresh cilantro leaves, packed
2 Tbsps. fresh mint leaves
¼ small sweet yellow onion

Add to the blender or processor and blend until smooth:

3 Tbsp. rice vinegar
3 Tbsp. sweetener of your choice
2 Tbsp. oil
¼ lb. tofu
pinch dried red pepper flakes

Shred:

½ lb. Napa or green cabbage
¼ lb. red cabbage
1 carrot

Mix all together and serve topped with.

1 Tbsp. toasted sesame seeds

Per Serving: Calories: 155, Protein: 3 gm., Fat: 9 gm., Carbohydrates: 14 gm.

Salad Sans Poulet

Makes about 3 cups

Freeze, thaw, squeeze dry and chop:
1 lb. tofu

Mix together in a bowl with:
⅓ cup onion, minced
⅓ cup celery, minced
1 Tbsp. nutritional yeast
1 Tbsp. fresh parsley, minced
1 clove garlic, minced or
½ tsp. garlic powder
½ tsp. poultry seasoning
¼ tsp. black pepper

Add and mix in:
1½ cups Tofu Salad Dressing, p. 42

Serve on lettuce or in sandwiches.

Per ½ Cup Serving: Calories: 181, Protein: 11 gm., Fat: 13 gm., Carbohydrates: 8 gm.

Tofu Lentil Salad

Serves 6

Have ready:
2 cups cooked and drained lentils

Dressing

Mix together well:
2 Tbsp. oil
2 Tbsp. vinegar
1 tsp. curry powder
½ tsp. salt
¼ tsp. black pepper

Salad

Mix together in a bowl:
¾ lb. tofu, crumbled
the lentils

Stir in the dressing along with:
2 Tbsp. onion, diced
½ cup celery, diced
½ cup carrot, grated
¼ cup sweet pickle relish
1 tsp. curry powder
1 tsp. salt

Chill and serve.

Per Serving: Calories: 176, Protein: 10 gm., Fat: 7 gm., Carbohydrates: 20 gm.

Potato Tofu Salad

Have ready:
**6 medium potatoes, cooked and peeled
(about 6 cups cooked and cubed)**

In large mixing bowl, put:

1 cup tofu, crumbled
the cooked, cubed potatoes
1 cup celery, cut in ¼" pieces

½ cup red onion, chopped fine
½ cup sweet pickle relish
1½ tsp. salt

Dressing

Blend in a blender or food processor until smooth and creamy:

1 cup tofu
2 Tbsp. oil
½ tsp. salt
1½ Tbsp. cider vinegar

½ Tbsp. lemon juice
⅛ tsp. garlic powder
dash black pepper
1 Tbsp. salad mustard

Add dressing to the salad and mix gently. Chill and serve.

Per Serving: Calories: 157, Protein: 8 gm., Fat: 5 gm., Carbohydrates: 31 gm.

Picnic Potato Salad

Scrub well and cut up:
4 medium potatoes

Boil in salted water until tender. Drain and pull skins off.

While still hot, toss with a mix of:

1 Tbsp. oil
1 Tbsp. vinegar
½ tsp. salt

⅛ tsp. black pepper
⅛ tsp. dry mustard

Let cool. Add to the cooled potatoes:

⅓ cup onion, minced
1 cup celery, diced

2 Tbsp. parsley, minced
celery salt to taste

Dressing

Blend in a blender or food processor until smooth and creamy:

¾ cup tofu, mashed
2 Tbsp. vinegar
1 Tbsp. oil

Mix in dressing, chill and serve.

Per Serving: Calories: 105, Protein: 4 gm., Fat: 5 gm., Carbohydrates: 14 gm.

Tabouli

Serves 12
Makes 6 cups

Soak together for one hour:
   2 cups boiling water
   1 cup bulgur wheat

Drain well. Add and mix into the drained bulgur:
   1 cup fresh parsley, chopped fine
   ½ cup fresh mint, chopped fine
   ½ lb. tofu, chopped fine
   2 tomatoes, chopped
   ½ cup black olives, chopped
   ¼ cup fresh lemon juice
   ¼ cup scallions, chopped
   2 Tbsp. olive oil
   ½ tsp. salt
   ¼ tsp. black pepper, freshly ground

Serve on a bed of leaf lettuce garnished with tomato wedges.

Per ½ Cup Serving: Calories: 157, Protein: 5 gm., Fat: 1 gm., Carbohydrates: 24 gm.

Tabouli Salad

Kanten Fruit and Vegetable Salad

Serves 6-8
Makes one 4½ cup mold

Dissolve and simmer for 5 minutes:
- **3 cups apricot nectar**
- **3 Tbsp. kanten flakes**

Set aside to cool. Mix together with the cooled kanten mixture:

- **½ lb. tofu, blended**
- **3 Tbsp. honey or sweetener of your choice**
- **¾ cup walnuts or pecans**

- **1½ cups carrots, shredded**
- **½ cup golden raisins**
- **½ tsp. vanilla**

Pour into the mold or individual serving dishes. Chill until firm (about 4-6 hours or overnight). Remove from the mold and serve.

Per Serving: Calories: 239, Protein: 6 gm., Fat: 8 gm., Carbohydrates: 36 gm.

Cucumber-Tomato Salad

Serves 6-8

Mix together in a salad bowl:

- **4 cups cumcumbers, sliced**
- **3 cups tomatoes, chopped**
- **⅔ cup onion, chopped**

- **1 cup celery, chopped**
- **½ cup parsley, chopped**

Dressing

Blend in a blender or food processor until smooth.

- **¼ lb. tofu, mashed**
- **3 Tbsp. lime juice**
- **1 Tbsp. oil**

- **1 tsp. sugar or sweetener of your choice**
- **½ tsp. salt**
- **¼ tsp. pepper**

Mix dressing and vegetables and serve.

Per Serving: Calories: 111, Protein: 6 gm., Fat: 3 gm., Carbohydrates: 9 gm.

Frozen Fruit Salad

Serves 6-8
Makes 1½ quarts

Blend in a blender or food processor until smooth and creamy:

- **1 lb. tofu**
- **¼ cup honey**
- **¼ cup lemon juice**

- **2 Tbsp. oil**
- **½ tsp. salt**

Fold into:

- **4 cups drained fruit, fresh or canned**
- **½ cup pecans, chopped**

- **2 tsp. crystallized ginger, chopped**

Pour into individual serving dishes and freeze. Thaw for 15 minutes before serving.

Per Serving: Calories: 258, Protein: 6 gm., Fat: 8 gm., Carbohydrates: 35 gm.

Apple-Nut Salad

Mix together:
   4 tart red apples, chopped
   2 cups celery, diced
   ½ cup pecans, chopped
   ¼ cup fresh lemon juice

Pour boiling water to cover:
   ½ cup raisins

Drain and add to the salad, then stir in:
   1½ cups Tofu Sour Creme Dressing, p. 41

Chill and serve.

Per Serving: Calories: 233, Protein: 5 gm., Fat: 10 gm., Carbohydrates: 26 gm.

Tofu Salad No. 1

This is good either as a sandwich spread or scooped on a piece of lettuce with tomato and garnished with parsley.

Mix together:
   1½ lbs. tofu, crumbled or mashed
   ½ cup Tofu Salad Dressing, p. 42
   ½ cup parsley, chopped
   ¼ cup pickle relish
   ½ medium onion, chopped fine
   2 stalks celery, chopped fine
   1½ tsp. garlic powder
   1½ tsp. salt
   ½ tsp. paprika
   ¼ tsp. black pepper

Per Serving: Calories: 130, Protein: 10 gm., Fat: 7 gm., Carbohydrates: 9 gm.

Tofu Salad No. 2

Mash or crumble into a bowl:
   1 lb. tofu

Mix in:
   ½ cup Tofu Salad Dressing, p. 42
   ⅓ cup celery, chopped fine
   1 Tbsp. fresh parsley, minced
   2 tsp. prepared mustard
   1 tsp. onion powder
   1 tsp. salt
   ½ tsp. garlic powder
   ½ tsp. black pepper
   ½ tsp. paprika
   ¼ tsp. tumeric

Serve as a sandwich spread or on lettuce or tomato as a salad. Also good stuffed into a fresh bell pepper or ripe avocado as a salad.

Per Serving: Calories: 82, Protein: 7 gm., Fat: 5 gm., Carbohydrates: 3 gm.

Lettuce Rolls

Serves 6-8
Makes 24 rolls

Prepare Tofu Salad Dressing, p. 42

Put in a mixing bowl:
1 lb. tofu, mashed
½ cup pitted black olives, sliced
¼ cup sweet relish (optional)

3 green onions, chopped fine
2 stalks celery, chopped fine

Mix well and add:
1½ cups Tofu Salad Dressing

Wash and dry the large outside leaves of a head of lettuce. Remove the stiff core piece from the leaves. Place ¼ cup tofu mixture along one side of leaf and roll up. Cut each roll in 3" sections and use toothpicks to keep roll snug.

Per Serving: Calories: 145, Protein: 8 gm., Fat: 8 gm., Carbohydrates: 5 gm.

Roberta's Tofu Salad

Makes 3½ cups

Mix together:
1 lb. tofu, crumbled
⅓ cup onion, finely chopped
⅓ cup celery, finely chopped
¾ cup Tofu Salad Dressing, p. 42

2 Tbsp. toasted sesame seeds
4 tsp. pickle relish
1 tsp. salt
½ tsp. dill weed

Serve on lettuce as salad or in sandwiches.

Per ½ Cup Serving: Calories: 104, Protein: 7 gm., Fat: 6 gm., Carbohydrates: 5 gm.

Cottage Tofu Salad

Serves 6-8
Makes 3 cups

Mix together:
1 lb. tofu, mashed or crumbled
1 Tbsp. fresh parsley

1½ tsp. dried chives
¼ tsp. dill weed

Blend in a blender until smooth and creamy:
½ cup tofu
2 Tbsp. oil
1½ tsp. vinegar

1½ tsp. lemon juice
1 tsp. salt
¼-½ tsp. black pepper

Pour this into the mashed tofu mixture and mix well. Serve either as a sandwich spread or on lettuce or tomato as a salad.

Per Serving: Calories: 96, Protein: 6 gm., Fat: 7 gm., Carbohydrates: 2 gm.

Salad Dressings And Sauces

Clockwise from top left: Russian Dressing, Cucumber Salad Dressing, Thousand Island Dressing, Green Goddess Dressing, Dill Salad Dressing

SALAD DRESSINGS AND SAUCES

Salad dressings and sauces come out best with the very soft or "silken" type of tofu. Soft Japanese-style tofu will also work fine. You will get the smoothest dressing or sauce if you use a blender. Read "Blending Tofu" on p. 7. If you don't have a blender, you can use a food processor, electric mixer, or even a wire whip, resulting is varying degrees of smooth and creamy consistency. Use only very fresh tofu for salad dressings and sauces. If you are calorie-conscious, you can leave the oil out of any recipe and still have a creamy, tasty dressing.

Thousand Island Dressing

Makes 1¾ cups

Combine in a blender and blend until smooth and creamy:

½ lb. tofu, mashed
½ cup ketchup
2 Tbsp. oil

½ tsp. onion powder
¼ tsp. salt
⅛ tsp. garlic powder

Fold in:

3 Tbsp. sweet pickle relish
3 Tbsp. stuffed green olives, minced
1 Tbsp. parsley, chopped fine

Per 1 Tbsp. Serving: Calories: 23, Protein: 1 gm., Fat: 1 gm., Carbohydrates: 2 gm.

Dill Salad Dressing

Makes 1¼ cups

Combine in a blender:

½ lb. tofu, mashed
1 Tbsp. oil
1 Tbsp. vinegar

½ tsp. dill weed
½ tsp. salt
⅛ tsp. black pepper

Blend until smooth and creamy.

Per 1 Tbsp. Serving: Calories: 15, Protein: 1 gm., Fat: 1 gm., Carbohydrates: 0 gm.

Cucumber Salad Dressing

Makes 1¾ cups

Combine in a blender:

½ lb. tofu, mashed
1 medium cucumber, peeled
2 Tbsp. oil

2 Tbsp. vinegar
½ tsp. salt
⅛ tsp. black pepper

Blend until smooth and creamy.

Per 1 Tbsp. Serving: Calories: 15, Protein: 1 gm., Fat: 1 gm., Carbohydrates: 0 gm.

Green Goddess Dressing

A San Francisco favorite with salad greens and avocado.

Combine in a blender:

½ lb. tofu, mashed	1 tsp. onion powder
2 Tbsp. oil	½ tsp. salt
½ Tbsp. dry chives	¼ tsp. garlic powder
¼ cup fresh parsley	⅛ tsp. black pepper
2 Tbsp. vinegar	

Blend until smooth and creamy.

Per 1 Tbsp. Serving: Calories: 15, Protein: 1 gm., Fat: 1 gm., Carbohydrates: 0 gm.

Creamy Italian Dressing

Combine in a blender:
- ½ lb. tofu
- 2 Tbsp. oil
- 2 Tbsp. vinegar
- 1 tsp. salt
- ⅛ tsp. freshly ground black pepper

Blend until smooth and creamy.

Fold in:
- 4 cloves garlic, minced
- 2 Tbsp. sweet pickle relish (optional)
- ¼ tsp. oregano
- ⅛ tsp. red pepper flakes

Per 1 Tbsp. Serving: Calories: 21, Protein: 1 gm., Fat: 2 gm., Carbohydrates: 0 gm.

Russian Dressing

Combine in a blender:

½ lb. soft tofu	1 Tbsp. prepared mustard
⅓ cup ketchup	1 tsp. onion powder
2 Tbsp. vinegar	½ tsp. salt
2 Tbsp. oil	

Blend until smooth and creamy.

Per 1 Tbsp. Serving: Calories: 21, Protein: 1 gm., Fat: 2 gm., Carbohydrates: 1 gm.

Creamy Sweet-Sour Fruit Salad Dressing

Makes about 2 cups

Combine in a blender or food processor:

½ cup tofu
½ cup apple cider vinegar
⅓ cup honey or
  sweetener of your choice
¼ cup oil

2 Tbsp. onion, minced
2 Tbsp. poppy seed
1½ tsp. dry mustard
1 tsp. salt
1 tsp. paprika

Blend until smooth and creamy.

Per 1 Tbsp. Serving: Calories: 32, Protein: 0 gm., Fat: 2 gm., Carbohydrates: 3 gm.

Sweet-Spicy Fruit Salad Dressing

Makes 1¾ cups

Combine in a blender:

½ lb. tofu, mashed
¼ cup lemon juice
¼ cup honey or
  sweetener of your choice

2 Tbsp. oil
¼ tsp. cinnamon
¼ tsp. vanilla
⅛ tsp. salt

Blend until smooth and creamy.

Per 1 Tbsp. Serving: Calories: 24, Protein: 1 gm., Fat: 1 gm., Carbohydrates: 3 gm.

Tofu Sour Creme Dressing

Makes about 1 cup

A versatile recipe you'll use again and again.

Combine in a blender:

½ lb. tofu
2 Tbsp. oil
1 Tbsp. fresh lemon juice

1½ tsp. sweetener of your choice
½ tsp. salt

Blend until smooth and creamy.

Per 1 Tbsp. Serving: Calories: 28, Protein: 1 gm., Fat: 2 gm., Carbohydrates: 1 gm.

Creamy Sweet-Sour Fruit Salad Dressing

Tofu Salad Dressing

Makes about 1½ cups

A basic creamy dressing for salads and sandwiches.

Combine in a blender:

½ lb. soft tofu
2 Tbsp. safflower oil
2 Tbsp. apple cider vinegar

1 Tbsp. sweetener of your choice
½ tsp. salt

Blend until smooth and creamy. You may have to add a little water if you are using a firmer tofu.

Per 1 Tbsp. Serving: Calories: 23, Protein: 1 gm., Fat: 2 gm., Carbohydrates: 1 gm.

Avocado Salad Dressing

Makes 1¼ cups

Combine in a blender:

1 ripe avocado (about ¾ cup)
½ cup Tofu Salad Dressing, p. 42
1 Tbsp. fresh lemon juice
½ tsp. salt
¼ tsp. garlic powder
⅛ tsp. black pepper

Blend until smooth and creamy.

Per 1 Tbsp. Serving: Calories: 24, Protein: 0 gm., Fat: 1 gm., Carbohydrates: 1 gm.

Tartare Sauce

Makes 2½ cups

Combine in a blender until smooth and creamy:

½ lb. tofu, mashed
¼ cup vinegar
2 Tbsp. oil

2 Tbsp. sweetener of your choice
1 tsp. prepared mustard
¾ tsp. salt

Fold in:

½ cup onion, chopped
¼ cup sweet pickle relish

Per 1 Tbsp. Serving: Calories: 16, Protein: 0 gm., Fat: 1 gm., Carbohydrates: 1 gm.

Hollandaise Sauce

Makes 1½ cups

Combine in a blender until smooth and creamy:

½ lb. tofu

¼ cup oil

¼ cup fresh lemon juice

½ tsp. sweetener of your choice

½ tsp. salt

⅛ tsp. black pepper

a few grains cayenne

This can be heated and served hot, but be careful not to let it boil.

Per 1 Tbsp. Serving: Calories: 29, Protein: 1 gm., Fat: 3 gm., Carbohydrates: 1 gm.

Horseradish Sauce

Makes 1 cup

Combine in a blender until smooth and creamy:

½ cup tofu, mashed

3 Tbsp. prepared horseradish

1 Tbsp. oil

1 Tbsp. vinegar

1 tsp. sweetener of your choice

½ tsp. salt

Per 1 Tbsp. Serving: Calories: 15, Protein: 1 gm., Fat: 1 gm., Carbohydrates: 1 gm.

Silken Miso Sauce

Makes 1½ cups

This can be served hot or cold over vegetables.

Combine in a blender until smooth and creamy:

1 (10.5 oz.) pkg. silken tofu

3 Tbsp. apple cider vinegar

2 Tbsp. white or yellow miso

2 Tbsp. oil

1 tsp. honey

½ tsp. garlic powder

¼ tsp. black pepper

If you want to serve it hot, heat it, but don't boil.

Per 1 Tbsp. Serving: Calories: 21, Protein: 1 gm., Fat: 2 gm., Carbohydrates: 1 gm.

Main Dishes

Barbequed Tofu and Picnic Potato Salad

MAIN DISHES

10
8 star

Spaghetti Primavera

Serves 4-6

This recipe is pictured on p. 4.

Cut into 2″ x ½″ x ⅛″ pieces:
1 lb. firm tofu

Marinate the pieces for at least 2 hours in a mixture of:
2 Tbsp. soy sauce   **1 Tbsp. oil**
2 Tbsp. wine vinegar

Brown the marinated tofu pieces lightly in:
1 Tbsp. oil
the leftover marinade

Set aside.

Boil until almost tender in 1″ boiling water:
4 cups broccoli florets (fresh or frozen)
1 ½ cups peas (fresh or frozen)

Drain and reserve water.

Saute together:
1 Tbsp. oil   **1 cup fresh mushrooms, sliced**

Cook until tender in boiling water:
1 lb. spaghetti or vermicelli noodles

Sauce

Let bubble together gently over low heat for 3 minutes:
⅓ cup oil
⅓ cup unbleached white flour

Whisk in without making lumps:
3 cups liquid (reserved cooking water or soymilk)

Add:
½ cup fresh parsley, chopped   **½ tsp. garlic powder**
1 ½ tsp. salt   **⅛ tsp. cayenne**

Continue cooking over low heat and stirring until thickened and smooth. Add tofu, vegetables and mushrooms to the sauce and serve hot over the noodles.

Variation: Substitute 2 cups broccoli florets and 2 cups asparagus spears for the 4 cups broccoli florets.

Per Serving: Calories: 712, Protein: 25 gm., Fat: 26 gm., Carbohydrates: 93 gm.

Curried Cashew Tofu Over Noodles

Serves 4

Preheat oven to 350° F.

Freeze, thaw, squeeze out and cut into 1″ x ½″ x ¼″ pieces:
   1 lb. tofu

Mix together:
   ¼ cup water
   2 Tbsp. soy sauce
   1 Tbsp. cashew butter
   1 Tbsp. curry powder

   2 tsp. honey
   1 tsp. onion powder
   ¼ tsp. black pepper

Pour this over the tofu pieces and squeeze it in so all the liquid is absorbed.

Spread a cookie sheet with:
   1 Tbsp. oil

Lay the tofu pieces out on the sheet in one layer. Bake 15 minutes. Turn the pieces over and bake 10 minutes more.

While the tofu is baking, cook in boiling water until tender:
   8 oz. flat noodles

To prepare the sauce, whip together in a saucepan:
   3 cups water
   3 Tbsp. arrowroot or cornstarch

   3 tsp. vegetable broth powder

Cook over low heat and continue stirring until thickened. Add the baked tofu pieces and:
   ½ cup roasted cashews (or other nuts if you like)

Serve hot over noodles topped with:
   2 scallions, chopped

Per Serving: Calories: 491, Protein: 21 gm., Fat: 14 gm., Carbohydrates: 59 gm.

Tofu Burgers

8 stars

Makes six 3″ burgers

Mix and mash together in a bowl:
   1 lb. tofu
   ¼ cup wheat germ
   ¼ cup whole wheat flour
   2 Tbsp. nutritional yeast

   1 Tbsp. grated onion
   ½ tsp. garlic powder
   ½ tsp. poultry seasoning
   ¼ tsp. black pepper

Form into six 3″ burgers. Brown on each side in:
   1 Tbsp. oil

Serve hot on a bun either plain or with all the fixings.

Per Burger: Calories: 119, Protein: 8 gm., Fat: 6 gm., Carbohydrates: 9 gm.

Sesame Tofu

Serves 4-6

Preheat oven to 350° F.

Cut into ¾" cubes or ¼" slices:
1 lb. firm tofu

Grind together in a food processor:
⅓ cup sesame seeds   **⅓ cup unbleached white flour**

Pour into a bowl.

Chop in a food processor:
1" cube ginger root   **2 cloves garlic**

Add and process until blended:
2 Tbsp. soy sauce   **2 Tbsp. water**

Dip each slice in the sauce, then dredge in the flour-sesame mixture. Arrange on a cookie sheet spread with:
1 Tbsp. oil

Sprinkle any leftover sauce over slices, then any leftover flour mixture. Bake 20 minutes on one side, then flip and bake 10 minutes on the other. Serve hot with rice.

Per Serving: Calories: 179, Protein: 10 gm., Fat: 7 gm., Carbohydrates: 10 gm.

Tofu Spinach Pie

Serves 6-8
Makes one 9" pie

Preheat oven to 400° F.

Have ready:
   1 (10 oz.) pkg. frozen chopped spinach, thawed and drained or
   1 lb. fresh spinach, chopped
   1 partially baked 9" pie shell

Saute together over low heat until soft:
   1 Tbsp. olive oil
   1½ cups chopped onion

Add and saute for 2 more minutes:
   the spinach

Mix all together with:
   1 lb. tofu, mashed or crumbled   **1 tsp. salt**
   1 Tbsp. lemon juice   **½ tsp. garlic powder**

Pour into the partially baked pie shell. Bake for about 30 minutes, or until crust is golden.

Per Serving: Calories: 188, Protein: 8 gm., Fat: 11 gm., Carbohydrates: 15 gm.

Seaside Cakes

Serves 6

Let bubble together over low heat for 1-2 minutes:

¼ cup oil   **¼ cup unbleached white flour**

Whip in slowly, leaving no lumps:

1 cup soymilk   **½ tsp. salt**

Stir in and continue cooking until very thick:

2 Tbsp. onion, minced

Combine in a bowl:

1 lb. tofu, crumbled   **½ tsp. dry mustard**
1 tsp. salt   **dash of cayenne**

Mix the white sauce into the tofu mix. Chill 3-4 hours. Shape the chilled mixture into cakes 2½" round by ½" thick.

Then roll cakes in a mixture of:

12-16 soda crackers, crushed to crumbs   **1½ tsp. paprika**

Chill the crumb-covered cakes about 1 hour. (At this point the cakes can be frozen for later use.)

Fry the cakes in:

2-3 Tbsp. oil per pan

Turn them gently, browning on both sides. Serve with lemon wedges, tartare sauce, or cocktail sauce and garnish with parsley or watercress.

Per Serving: Calories: 313, Protein: 8 gm., Fat: 27 gm., Carbohydrates: 11 gm.

Chili Con Tofu

Makes 2 quarts

This is American-style chili with tomato broth.

Have ready:

2½ cups cooked pinto beans   **water or stock to cover**

Stir together in a bowl:

1 lb. tofu, crumbled   **1 Tbsp. soy sauce**

Saute together in a soup pot until tofu is browned·

2 Tbsp. oil   **2 cloves garlic, minced**
1 medium onion, chopped   **the tofu-soy sauce mixture**
½ green pepper, chopped

Add to the pot:

1 (16 oz.) can tomato sauce   **1½ Tbsp. chili powder**
1 cup water or stock

Bring to a boil and serve.

Per 1 Cup Serving: Calories: 180, Protein: 11 gm., Fat: 6 gm., Carbohydrates: 22 gm.

Chili Con Tofu With Beans

Makes 1½ quarts

This is southwestern-style chili made with frozen tofu and a chili broth.

Have ready:
2½ cups cooked pinto beans
enough water to cover
1 lb. frozen tofu, thawed, squeezed dry,
    and torn into bite-size pieces

Preheat over to 350° F.

Whip together:
¼ cup water
2 Tbsp. soy sauce
1 Tbsp. peanut butter
1 tsp. onion powder
½ tsp. cumin
¼ tsp. garlic powder

Pour this over the prepared tofu pieces and squeeze in so all liquid is absorbed evenly. Spread a cookie sheet with:
1 Tbsp. oil

Spread the tofu pieces on the oiled cookie sheet and bake 20 minutes, flip them over and bake 10 minutes on the other side.

Saute in a heavy soup pot until tender:
1 Tbsp. oil
1 large green pepper, diced
1 large onion, diced
2 cloves garlic, minced

Add to the pot:
the cooked beans and water
1 Tbsp. chili powder
1 tsp. cumin
1 tsp. salt
the baked tofu pieces

Bring to a simmer and serve hot with Sesame Tofu Crackers, p. 121, and salad.

Per 1 Cup Serving: Calories: 231, Protein: 14 gm., Fat: 8 gm., Carbohydrates: 25 gm.

Chili Con Tofu With Beans

Tofu Rancheros

This is an adaptation of a classic Mexican dish that is traditionally served for breakfast with refried pinto beans and sweet coffee. The "ranchero" sauce derives its name from being made rapidly in one frying pan, as if over an open fire "en un rancho."

Prepare vegetables and set aside:
3 large or 4 medium ripe tomatoes, wedged
1 large onion, chopped

2 cloves garlic, chopped
¼ cup fresh cilantro or parsley, chopped

Slice into eight slices and sprinkle with a little salt:
1 lb. firm tofu

In a heavy skillet, heat over medium heat:
2 Tbsp. oil

Fry in the hot oil for 2 seconds on each side:
8 corn (masa) tortillas

The tortillas should be heated, but soft. Put 2 tortillas on each plate, side by side.

In the same pan, quickly brown the tofu slices on each side in:
1 Tbsp. oil

Put one slice on each tortilla. Immediately add to the hot pan:
chopped onion   **chopped garlic**

Stir and fry until they start to brown, then add to the pan:
the tomato wedges

Stir, cover, and steam for 3 minutes, then add:
1 (6 oz.) can chopped green chilies   **salt to taste**
a pinch of ground cumin

Stir, cover and steam for 3 more minutes. When the tomatoes are soft and saucy, but before they lose their shape completely, remove from heat and pour equally over the plates with tortillas and tofu. Serve immediately, garnished with the chopped cilantro or parsley.

Per Serving: Calories: 372, Protein: 15 gm., Fat: 13 gm., Carbohydrates: 36 gm.

Potato-Tofu Casserole

Preheat oven to 325° F.

Mix together in a bowl:
3 cups potatoes, mashed
1½ lbs. tofu, mashed
¼ cup fresh parsley, chopped

1¼ tsp. salt
¼ tsp. black pepper
¼ tsp. garlic powder

Saute together:
2 Tbsp. oil   **1 medium onion, chopped**

When onions are limp, mix into the potato-tofu mixture. Spread into an oiled 8″ x 8″ x 2″ baking dish, and sprinkle with paprika. Bake for 35 minutes.

Per Serving: Calories: 253, Protein: 11 gm., Fat: 17 gm., Carbohydrates: 4 gm.

Filet de Tofu

Tofu that smells slightly sour can be used in this recipe.

Cut into ½″ to ⅝″ slices:
2 lbs. tofu

Boil the slices in salted water for 20 minutes, adding a bit of seaweed to water if you like. Drain and let cool.

Preheat oven to 350° F.

Lay the slices out close together in a shallow pan and sprinkle with:
1 tsp. paprika   **1 tsp. salt**
2 Tbsp. parsley, minced   **½ tsp. black pepper**
1 tsp. chives, chopped fine

Carefully pour in and around the tofu pieces, not disturbing the herbs, until it reaches the top of the slices:
vegetable bouillon (about ¾ cup)

Bake for about 20 minutes or until almost all the liquid is gone. Remove pan from oven and pour more of the liquid on in the same manner as before. Bake another 10 minutes until liquid is almost gone again.

Brush with:
olive oil

Squeeze on:
fresh lemon juice to taste

Then broil until lightly browned. Serve garnished with parsley and lemon wedges.

Per Serving: Calories: 110, Protein: 10 gm., Fat: 7 gm., Carbohydrates: 3 gm.

Indonesian Satay

Chop in a food processor:
2 cloves garlic
1″ cube fresh ginger root, peeled

Add and process until smooth:
¼ cup boiling water   **½ tsp. ground coriander**
2 Tbsp. soy sauce   **½ tsp. vinegar or lemon juice**
2 Tbsp. peanut butter   **⅛ tsp. cayenne**
2 tsp. honey

Slice into ½″ slices:
1 lb. tofu

Spread on the bottom of an 8″ x 8″ pan:
1 Tbsp. oil

Pour a thin layer of sauce into the pan, then arrange the slices of tofu in a single layer. Pour over the rest of the sauce. Let sit to marinate at least one hour. Bake at 375° F. for 20-25 minutes. Serve with rice and vegetables.

Per Serving: Calories: 138, Protein: 9 gm., Fat: 8 gm., Carbohydrates: 6 gm.

Fresh Shiitake Stir-Fry

Serves 4

Chop together in a food processor:
1" cube fresh ginger, peeled
2 cloves fresh garlic

Add to the food processor and blend:
¼ cup mirin
2 Tbsp. soy sauce

Pour this over:
1 lb. firm tofu, cut in ½" cubes

Let this marinate while preparing vegetables below:
½ cup scallions, sliced
1 red bell pepper, cut in triangles
3½ oz. fresh shiitake mushrooms, sliced
½ lb. snow peas, washed and stems removed

Heat a wok with:
1 Tbsp. oil

Add scallions and peppers, stir-fry one minute. Add mushrooms and snow peas, stir-fry one minute. Add the tofu and marinade, stir-fry one minute, then cover and steam until hot. Serve over brown rice.

Per Serving: Calories: 188, Protein: 12 gm., Fat: 8 gm., Carbohydrates: 19 gm.

Apricot-Orange Barbeque

Serves 4-6

Preheat oven to 350° F.

Slice into ¼" slices:
1 lb. firm tofu

Lightly fry in:
1 Tbsp. oil

Arrange the fried slices in a baking dish. Saute together until transparent:
1 Tbsp. oil   **¼ cup onions, chopped**

Stir in:
6 Tbsp. apricot jam   **½ tsp. coriander**
5 Tbsp. frozen orange juice concentrate   **½ tsp. salt**
5 Tbsp. water   **½ tsp. ginger**
2 Tbsp. prepared mustard   **⅛ tsp. garlic powder**
1 Tbsp. vinegar   **1/16-⅛ tsp. cayenne (optional)**

Pour the sauce over the tofu and bake 10-15 minutes, until bubbling.

Per Serving: Calories: 236, Protein: 8 gm., Fat: 9 gm., Carbohydrates: 20 gm.

Fresh Shiitake Stir-Fry

Barbequed Tofu

Using frozen tofu lends a chewy texture. This recipe is pictured on p. 44.

Freeze, thaw, squeeze out, and cut into ½" thick strips:
   2 lbs. firm tofu

Preheat oven to 350° F.

Spread a cookie sheet with:
   2 Tbsp. oil

Arrange the tofu strips on the oiled cookie sheet.

Mix together:
   ¼ cup water   **½ tsp. garlic**
   2 Tbsp. peanut butter   **¼ tsp. black pepper**
   1 Tbsp. soy sauce

Pour this mixture evenly over the tofu strips and press into the strips with an open hand. Bake for about 15 minutes, then turn the pieces over and bake for about 10 minutes on the other side. Pour your favorite Barbeque Sauce (or see below) over all and bake 10 minutes more. Serve with French bread and salad.

Barbeque Sauce

Saute together until onions are transparent:
   2 Tbsp. oil
   1 medium onion, chopped
   2 cloves garlic, minced

Stir in:
   1 (15 oz.) can tomato sauce   **1 Tbsp. fresh parsley, chopped**
   ¾ cup brown sugar or   **or 1½ tsp. dried parsley**
     ½ cup honey   **1 tsp. allspice**
   ½ cup salad mustard   **1 tsp. crushed red pepper**
   ½ cup water   **or ½ tsp. cayenne pepper**
   1 Tbsp. molasses

Bring to a boil, reduce heat to a simmer and add:
   ½ cup lemon juice
     or ½ cup apple cider vinegar
   2 Tbsp. soy sauce

Simmer 10-15 minutes more.

Per Serving: Calories: 343, Protein: 14 gm., Fat: 15 gm., Carbohydrates: 40 gm.

Stir-Fry Chinese Cabbage and Tofu

Have ready:

1 lb. tofu, cut in 1" x ½" x ¼" pieces
1" square piece of ginger root, peeled and finely diced
¼ tsp. vegetarian bouillon, dissolved in 2 Tbsp. water
1½ tsp. cornstarch, mixed into 2 Tbsp. water
4 cups Chinese cabbage, chopped and separated into crunchy and leafy parts
2 cloves garlic, crushed

Cut the crunchy parts of the Chinese cabbage into 1" wide pieces. Cut leafy parts into small piec

Heat in a wok or heavy skillet:

1 Tbsp. oil

Add chopped ginger and one clove crushed garlic. Let them fry until brown, then remove. Ad
the sliced tofu and stir to cover all with the flavored oil.

Add:

1 Tbsp. soy sauce
¼ tsp. salt

Stir and cook for 2 minutes. Remove from pan with all juices.

In the same pan, heat:

1 Tbsp. oil

Add the other crushed garlic, fry until brown. Remove. Add the crunchy sections of the Chinese
cabbage and stir. Cook for 1 minute.

Add:

the dissolved bouillon
¼ tsp. salt

Cover and steam 2 minutes. Add the leafy sections of the cabbage and stir. Cover and cook for
1 minute. Return the tofu to the pan. Dribble the cornstarch mixture into the center of the pan
where the juices are, stir and cook until thickened and serve immediately.

Per Serving: Calories: 112, Protein: 8 gm., Fat: 8 gm., Carbohydrates: 4 gm.

Mushroom-Almond Tofu Over Noodles

Serves 4-6

Freeze, thaw, squeeze out, and cut into ½″ x ½″ x 1½″ pieces:
1 lb. tofu

Preheat oven to 350° F.

Mix together in a food processor or blender:

2 Tbsp. hot water　　　　　　　　**¼ tsp. garlic powder or**
2 Tbsp. soy sauce　　　　　　　　　**1 clove garlic**
2 Tbsp. almond butter　　　　　　**¼ tsp. black pepper**

Pour this over the tofu pieces and squeeze in so it is all absorbed equally.

Spread a cookie sheet with:
1 Tbsp. oil

Lay the tofu pieces on the cookie sheet. Bake for 15 minutes. Turn the pieces over and bake 10 minutes more. While they are baking, cook until tender:
12 oz. flat noodles

Prepare Mushroom Gravy below.

Dark Mushroom-Almond Gravy

Saute together:
1 Tbsp. oil　　　　　　　　　　　**½ cup almonds, sliced**
½ lb. fresh mushrooms, sliced　　**¼ cup fresh parsley, chopped**

Whisk together:
3 cups water or stock　　　　　　**1 Tbsp. soy sauce**
3 Tbsp. arrowroot or cornstarch

Pour this into the pan with mushrooms and almonds, and continue stirring over low heat until hot and thickened.

Arrange the baked tofu pieces on a platter of noodles, then pour the sauce over and serve.

Per Serving: Calories: 536, Protein: 22 gm., Fat: 17 gm., Carbohydrates: 63 gm.

Lasagne

Serves 8-10
Makes one 9″ x 13″ pan

Have ready:
3½-4 cups Basic Italian-Style Tomato Sauce, p. 65,
or ready-made tomato sauce
Ricotta-Style Filling, opposite page

Cook and drain:
½ lb. lasagne noodles

Preheat oven to 350° F.

Start making layers in a 9″ x 13″ pan, starting with a thin layer of tomato sauce, then a layer of cooked noodles, then a layer of half of the Ricotta-Style Filling. Continue in the same order, using half the remaining tomato sauce, noodles, the remaining tofu, and ending with the remaining tomato sauce. Bake for about 30 minutes.

Per Serving: Calories: 220, Protein: 11 gm., Fat: 4 gm., Carbohydrates: 32 gm.

Eggplant Lasagne

Wash, peel, and slice into ¼" pieces:
1 medium eggplant (about 1¼ lbs.)

Spread the slices out on racks or paper towels, then sprinkle with:
juice of ½ lemon
salt

Let stand for 5-10 minutes, then wipe off with paper towels.

While eggplant is standing, mix together in a bowl:
¼ cup unbleached flour
¼ cup cornmeal
½ tsp. oregano
½ tsp. garlic powder
⅛ tsp. black pepper

Preheat oven to 350° F.

Dredge the toweled eggplant slices in the flour-cornmeal mixture. Lay on a cookie sheet spread with:
2 Tbsp. oil

Oven-fry the slices for 8-10 minutes on each side or until golden brown.

Ricotta-Style Filling

While the eggplant slices are baking, prepare the tofu filling. Process in a food processor to a fine grainy texture like ricotta cheese:

1½ lbs. firm tofu	**2 tsp. honey**
¼ cup lemon juice	**1 tsp. salt**
2 tsp. dried basil or	**1 clove garlic or**
2 Tbsp. fresh chopped basil	**½ tsp. garlic powder**

Cover the bottom of an 8" x 8" pan with:
½ cup Italian-Style Tomato Sauce, pg. 65.

Use half the oven fried eggplant slices to cover the bottom of the pan. Then spread the tofu filling over, reserving ½ cup for the top. Next, cover the tofu filling with the rest of the eggplant slices and pour over the top:
1 cup Italian-Style Tomato Sauce

Arrange the reserved tofu mixture in small dollops over the top. Bake for about 45 minutes or until the dollops are slightly browned. Serve with a tossed green salad and garlic bread.

Per Serving. Calories: 310, Protein: 17 gm., Fat: 12 gm., Carbohydrates: 36 gm.

Mediterranean Spring Rolls

Makes 12 to 15

These can also be made smaller for appetizers.

Have ready:
   1 pkg. fillo, thawed

Mix together:
   1 lb. tofu, crumbled or mashed
   1 bunch fresh spinach, washed, stemmed and chopped (4 cups)
   ½ cups fresh green onions, chopped fine
   ¼ cup lemon juice
   2 Tbsp. fresh mint or
      2 tsp. dry mint
   1 Tbsp. fresh basil or
      1 tsp. dry basil
   1 clove fresh garlic, minced, or
      ¼ tsp. garlic powder
   1 tsp. salt
   ½ tsp. black pepper

Mix together:
   1 Tbsp. olive oil
   1 Tbsp. margarine, melted

Fold one sheet of fillo in half and brush lightly with the olive oil-margarine mixture. Fold in half again to form about a 4" square and put ⅓ to ½ cup of filling in the middle. Fold the four corners together like an envelope. Place on a lightly oiled cookie sheet and brush the top lightly with the oil-margarine mixture. Bake at 350° F for about 20 minutes or until lightly browned.

Per Spring Roll: Calories: 142, Protein: 7 gm., Fat: 3 gm., Carbohydrates: 28 gm.

Crunchy Tofu Cutlets or Sticks

Serves 6-8

Preheat oven to 400° F.

Freeze, thaw, and squeeze out:
   2 lbs. tofu

Or have ready:
   2 lbs. firm tofu

Cut the tofu into 1½" x 3" x ¾" pieces and marinate for 2 hours in:
   ¼ cup soy sauce

Roll each stick in a mixture of:

1 cup cracker crumbs	**1 tsp. garlic powder**
1 cup unbleached white flour	**2 tsp. parsley flakes**
1 tsp. salt	**½ tsp. turmeric**

Brush a cookie sheet with:
   2 Tbsp. oil

Lay the tofu pieces on the cookie sheet leaving about ½" between each piece. Bake for 15 minutes on each side. Serve with Tartare Sauce, p. 42, or cocktail sauce.

Per Serving: Calories: 219, Protein: 13 gm., Fat: 9 gm., Carbohydrates: 21 gm.

Tofu Loaf

Preheat oven to 350° F.

Mix together:
   1 lb. tofu, mashed
   ½ cup wheat germ
   ⅓ cup parsley, chopped
   ¼ cup onion, chopped
     or 1 Tbsp. onion powder
   2 Tbsp. soy sauce
   2 Tbsp. nutritional yeast (optional)
   ½ Tbsp. Dijon mustard
   ¼ tsp. garlic powder
   ¼ tsp. black pepper

Oil a loaf pan with:
   2 Tbsp. oil

Press the tofu mixture into the oiled loaf pan and bake for about 1 hour. Let cool about 10 minutes before removing from the pan. Garnish with ketchup and parsley. Also good sliced and fried for sandwiches the next day.

Per Serving: Calories: 120, Protein: 8 gm., Fat: 8 gm., Carbohydrates: 7 gm.

Tofu Loaf garnished with mashed potatoes

Tofu Foo Yung

Serves 6

In a skillet or wok, saute over low heat for about 5 minutes:
2 Tbsp. oil
1 cup snow peas, cut in 1" pieces
1 cup fresh mushrooms, sliced
8 green onions, cut in 1½" pieces
1 (8 oz.) can water chestnuts, sliced

When vegetables are crisp-tender, mix in:
2 cups fresh bean sprouts

Remove from heat and set aside.

Preheat oven to 325° F.

Blend until smooth and creamy:
1¾ lbs. tofu
2 Tbsp. soy sauce

Pour this into a bowl and mix in:
½ cup tofu, mashed
¾ cup unbleached white flour
3 Tbsp. nutritional yeast (optional)
2 tsp. baking powder

Mix vegetables and tofu mixture together well. On an oiled cookie sheet, make six to eight 5" rounds about ½" thick, using about ½ cup of the mixture for each round. Leave about 1" space between the rounds. Bake for 30 minutes, flip over and bake 15 minutes more. Serve hot over rice or noodles with Mushroom Gravy, below.

Mushroom Gravy

Mix together in a saucepan:
2 cups cold water
4 Tbsp. soy sauce
2 Tbsp. cornstarch
½ cup fresh mushrooms, diced small

Cook over low heat, stirring until thickened.

Per Serving: Calories: 262, Protein: 17 gm., Fat: 13 gm., Carbohydrates: 22 gm.

Tofu Foo Yung with Mushroom Gravy

Tofu Spaghetti Balls

Makes sixteen 1½" balls

Preheat oven to 350° F.

Mix together:

1 lb. tofu, mashed
½ cup wheat germ
¼ cup parsley, chopped
2 Tbsp. soy sauce
2 Tbsp. nutritional yeast (optional)

1 Tbsp. onion powder
½ tsp. garlic powder
¼ tsp. black pepper
¼ tsp. oregano

Spread an 8" x 8" pan with:

2 Tbsp. olive oil

Form mixture into sixteen 1½" balls and arrange in the pan. Bake about 30 minutes, turning carefully about every 10 minutes, until browned and set.

Per Spaghetti Ball: Calories: 50, Protein: 3 gm., Fat: 3 gm., Carbohydrates: 3 gm.

Tofu Spaghetti Balls

Basic Italian-Style Tomato Sauce

Makes 7 cups

Saute until tender:
- ¼ cup olive oil or canola oil
- 1 medium onion, chopped
- 1 medium green pepper, chopped
- 2 carrots, diced (2 cups)
- 2 celery stalks, diced (2 cups)
- ½ lb. mushrooms, sliced (optional)

Add:
- 6 cups (3-15 oz. cans) tomato sauce
- ½ cup fresh Italian parsley, chopped
- 2 Tbsp. wine vinegar
- 3 cloves garlic, minced
- 1 tsp. basil
- ½ tsp. oregano

Simmer over low heat 30 minutes. For a smoother sauce, process in a food processor or blender until smooth. This is a good way to sneak those vegetables into children who claim they won't eat them.

Per ½ Cup Serving: Calories: 94, Protein: 3 gm., Fat: 4 gm., Carbohydrates: 14 gm.

Greco-Italian Pasta With Tofu

Serves 4-6

Put on water sufficient to boil:
- ½ lb. elbow macaroni

Cut into ¼" cubes:
- 1 lb. firm tofu

Fry cubes until browned in:
- 1 Tbsp. olive oil

In another pan, simmer together for a couple of minutes:
- 1 Tbsp. olive oil
- 1 Tbsp. basil
- 1 Tbsp. oregano
- 1 Tbsp. parsley
- ½ tsp. salt

Blend together in a blender or with a whip:
- 1 cup water
- 2 Tbsp. unbleached flour, arrowroot or cornstarch

Stir this mixture slowly into the simmering herbs and continue stirring until thickened. Turn off the heat and stir in:
- 1 tsp. garlic granules
- ½ cup raisins
- ½ cup walnuts, coarsley chopped
- the browned tofu

Immediately toss into the macaroni and serve.

Per Serving: Calories: 410, Protein: 16 gm., Fat: 11 gm., Carbohydrates: 52 gm.

Enchiladas

(This recipe is featured on the cover.)

Enchiladas are traditionally served with refried pinto beans, Spanish rice and tossed salad. Adjust the amount of chili in the sauce to your own taste.

Freeze, thaw, squeeze dry, and tear or chop into bite-size pieces:
1½ lbs. tofu

Have ready:
12 masa (corn) tortillas or Flour Tortillas, p. 117

Prepare either Chili Gravy or Tomato Sauce below.

Chili Gravy

Saute together until transparent:
2 Tbsp. oil
1 large onion, chopped

Mix together in a separate bowl:
3-6 Tbsp. chili powder (to taste)   **1 tsp. garlic powder**
6 Tbsp. unbleached white flour   **1 tsp. salt**
1 Tbsp. cumin

Stir this into the sauteed onion, then whip in slowly without making lumps:
1½ qts. water or stock

Bring to a boil and simmer 20 minutes.

Tomato Sauce

Saute together:
2 Tbsp. oil
1 large onion, chopped
3 cloves garlic, minced

When onions are transparent, stir in:
2 (15 oz.) cans tomato sauce   **1 Tbsp. cumin**
2 cups water or stock   **1 tsp. salt**
3-6 Tbsp. chili powder

Simmer for 20 minutes.

While your sauce is simmering, preheat oven to 350° F, and whip together:
3 Tbsp. soy sauce   **2 tsp. onion powder**
1 Tbsp. peanut butter   **1 tsp. cumin**

Pour this over the prepared tofu and squeeze in evenly. Spread a cookie sheet with:
2 Tbsp. oil

Lay the tofu pieces evenly over the cookie sheet, and bake for 15 minutes.

(Enchiladas, continued on next page)

(Enchiladas, continued)

Pour a thin layer of Chili Gravy or Tomato Sauce into a 9" x 13" pan. Dunk a tortilla in the Gravy or Sauce, then lay it on a plate. Lay about ⅓ cup of the tofu filling across the tortilla and roll it up. Repeat for the rest of the tortillas. Arrange all the rolled up tortillas in the pan, and cover with the rest of the Chili Gravy or Tomato Sauce. Bake for about 20 to 25 minutes or until bubbling.

Serve with a dollop of Cilantro-Jalapeno Dip, p. 13

Variation: Before baking, sprinkle over the top:
   ¾ cup onions, chopped
   ¾ cup black olives, choppped

Per Serving (With Chili Gravy): Calories: 302, Protein: 12 gm., Fat: 14 gm., Carbohydrates: 34 gm.

Per Serving (With Tomato Sauce): Calories: 336, Protein: 14 gm., Fat: 14 gm., Carbohydrates: 59 gm.

Walnut Broccoli Stir-Fry
Serves 6

Cut and brown lightly:
   1 lb. firm tofu, cut into 1" cubes   **2 Tbsp. oil**

Bring to a boil:
   1 cup water   **½ tsp. salt**

Drop into boiling salted water, boil one minute, drain and reserve the liquid:
   2 carrots, sliced thin
   2 cups broccoli florets, with 1" or 2" stems

In a wok or large frying pan, saute over medium heat until soft:
   1 Tbsp. oil   **2 onions, thinly sliced**

Then add:
   1 cup mushrooms, sliced   **½-1 cup walnut halves**

Increase heat to medium high and add the carrots and broccoli. Stir. Add tofu cubes, stir again.

To the reserved vegetable stock, add:
   1 Tbsp. cornstarch   **½ tsp. freshly ground black pepper**
   3 Tbsp. soy sauce

Pour over the vegetables and tofu, then stir and cook everything until bubbling. Serve hot over rice or Chinese noodles.

Per Serving: Calories: 245, Protein: 12 gm., Fat: 16 gm., Carbohydrates: 16 gm.

Tamale Pie

Freeze, thaw, squeeze out, and cut or tear into bite-size pieces:
1 lb. tofu

Saute together until soft:
1 Tbsp. oil
1 large onion, chopped (1 cup)
1 large bell pepper, chopped (1 cup)
¼ cup fresh cilantro, chopped
1 clove garlic, minced

When these are almost soft, stir in:
the prepared tofu in bite-size pieces
1 (15 oz.) can tomatoes, chopped
1 (15 oz.) can tomato sauce
2 Tbsp. chili powder
2 tsp. cumin
½ tsp. oregano
1 cup (½ can) black olives (optional)
1 (10 oz.) pkg. frozen cut corn
1 (6 oz.) can green chilis, chopped

Pour into a 9″ x 13″ baking dish.

Preheat oven to 350° F. Prepare Cornbread Topping below.

Cornbread Topping

Mix together in a bowl:
1 cup cornmeal
1 cup whole wheat flour
2 tsp. baking powder
½ tsp. salt

Stir together and pour into the dry ingredients:
1 cup soymilk
2 Tbsp. oil
1 Tbsp. honey or sweetener of your choice

Pour this over the top of the filling in the baking pan and bake for about 45 minutes, or until cornbread is browned.

Per Serving: Calories: 309, Protein: 13 gm., Fat: 10 gm., Carbohydrates: 45 gm.

Tofu Pot Pie

Have ready:
   Top crust from your favorite recipe to fit a 2 quart casserole

Filling

Freeze, thaw, squeeze dry, and cut into ½" cubes:
   1 lb. tofu

Parboil for 10 minutes and save the cooking water from:
   1 cup potatoes, cut in ½" cubes
   1 cup carrots, sliced or cut in ½" cubes

Have ready:
   1 cup shelled peas, fresh or frozen

Saute together:
   1 Tbsp. oil
   1 medium onion, chopped
   1 clove garlic, minced
   ½ tsp. salt

When the onions are soft, add the tofu cubes, parboiled vegetables and peas, and continue to simmer while preparing the gravy.

Preheat the oven to 350° F.

Gravy

Let bubble together over low heat for about a minute:
   3 Tbsp. oil
   3 Tbsp. whole wheat flour
   3 Tbsp. nutritional yeast

Whisk in:

1½ cups vegetable cooking water	**½ tsp. thyme**
1½ cups soymilk	**½ tsp. garlic powder**
1 tsp. salt	**½ tsp. black pepper**
1 tsp. sage	**½ tsp. paprika**

Heat and stir with the whisk until boiling and thickened. Mix the tofu-vegetable mixture and the gravy together in a 2 quart casserole and cover with the pie crust. Bake for 30-40 minutes or until the crust is golden.

Per Serving: Calories: 302, Protein: 11 gm., Fat: 18 gm., Carbohydrates: 25 gm.

Manicotti or Herbed Stuffed Shells

Serves 4-6

Either filling can be stuffed into manicotti noodles or jumbo macaroni shells. The manicotti look especially attractive made with homemade spinach noodles.

Have ready:
>   4 oz. (about 7) manicotti noodles cooked to al-dente
>   or 6 oz. jumbo macaroni shells cooked to al-dente
>   or ½ recipe of Noodles or Spinach Noodles, p. 123 cut to manicotti size (about 7-4" x
>   6" pieces) and cooked to al-dente (3-4 minutes)
>   1 lb. ready made pasta sauce
>   or about 2 cups Italian-Style Tomato Sauce, p. 65
>   one of the fillings below

Spinach Filling

Have ready:
>   1 lb. fresh spinach, washed and chopped
>   or 1 (10 oz.) pkg. frozen chopped spinach, thawed and drained

Saute together:
>   2 Tbsp. olive oil   1 medium onion, chopped

When onions are translucent, stir in the spinach and turn off the heat.

Mix together in a bowl:
>   1 lb. tofu, mashed   ½ tsp. garlic powder
>   2 Tbsp. lemon juice   ¼ tsp. black pepper
>   1 tsp. salt

Add the spinach-onion mixture to this and stir until well mixed.

Herbed Filling

Saute together until onions are transparent:
>   1 Tbsp. olive oil   ½ medium green pepper, chopped
>   1 medium onion, chopped   ¼ cup fresh parsley, chopped

Blend in a food processor until creamy:
>   1 lb. tofu   ½ tsp. garlic powder
>   2 Tbsp. lemon juice   ½ tsp. basil
>   1 tsp. salt   ¼ tsp. oregano

Stir all together.

Preheat oven to 350° F. Pour a thin layer of your choice of tomato sauce on the bottom of a 6" x 10" pan for manicotti or a 9" x 13" pan for shells. Fill each cooked noodle with your choice of filling. For the homemade noodles, lay the filling across the shorter end of the noodle and roll it up. Line the filled noodles up in the pan and cover with the rest of the tomato sauce. Cover the pan to keep the noodles from drying out. Bake for about 30 minutes, or until bubbling, and serve.

Per Serving (Spinach Filling): Calories: 342, Protein: 16 gm., Fat: 11 gm., Carbohydrates: 42 gm.

Per Serving (Herbed Filling): Calories: 304, Protein: 14 gm., Fat: 9 gm., Carbohydrates: 39 gm.

Almond Tofu

Serves 4-6

Have ready:
½ cup roasted almonds

Cut into ¾″ pieces:
2 lbs. firm tofu

Whip together, then mix with the tofu cubes:

¼ cup soy sauce	**1 tsp. onion powder**
1 Tbsp. peanut butter	**¼ tsp. garlic powder**

Brown the tofu over medium heat until liquid is absorbed in:
2 Tbsp. oil

In another pan, saute together only until crisp-tender:

1 Tbsp. oil	**1 (8 oz.) can water chestnuts, sliced and**
1 large bell pepper, cut in 1″ squares	**drained**
6-8 green onions, cut in 1½″ pieces	**1 Tbsp. fresh ginger root, grated**
3 stalks celery, cut in 1″ pieces	**or 1 Tbsp. powdered ginger**

While the vegetables are cooking, shake together in a jar or blend in a blender:

2 cups cold water	**2 Tbsp. cornstarch**
¼ cup soy sauce	

When the vegetables are crisp-tender, pour the mixture over them and continue simmering until thickened. Add the browned tofu and roasted almonds. Mix together well and serve over rice.

Variation: Replace almonds with roasted cashews for Cashew Tofu.

Per Serving: Calories: 374, Protein: 21 gm., Fat: 19 gm., Carbohydrates: 22 gm.

Almond Tofu

Fajitas

Have ready:
    1 lb. tofu, frozen, thawed, and squeezed dry
    4-6 flour tortillas
    1 tomato, chopped
    2-3 cups lettuce, chopped
    Cilantro-Jalapeno Dip, p. 13
    ½ green pepper, sliced
    ½ red onion, sliced

Preheat oven to 350° F.

Cut the tofu into 1" x ½" x ¼" pieces and put them in a bowl. Mix together in another bowl:
    ¼ cup water
    2 Tbsp. soy sauce
    1 Tbsp. peanut butter
    1 tsp. onion powder
    ½ tsp. cumin
    ¼ tsp. garlic powder
    ¼ tsp. black pepper

Pour this mixture over the tofu pieces and squeeze in evenly.

Spread a cookie sheet with:
    1 Tbsp. oil

Lay the tofu pieces out evenly over half the cookie sheet and bake for 15 minutes, and turn them over. Lay the green pepper and onion slices on the other half of the cookie sheet and bake 10 more minutes.

Heat each tortilla on a hot griddle. Divide the tofu, peppers and onions among the tortillas. Top with chopped tomato, lettuce and a dollop (1-2 Tbsp.) of Cilanto-Jalapeno Dip. Fold up and enjoy.

Per Fajita: Calories: 181, Protein: 11 gm., Fat: 7 gm., Carbohydrates: 18 gm.

Scrambled Tofu

A fast breakfast dish, or quick hot protein for any meal.

Saute until tender:
    1 Tbsp. oil
    ½ cup onion, chopped

Add to the pan:
    1 lb. tofu, crumbled   1 tsp. basil or cilantro
    1 Tbsp. soy sauce   ¼ tsp. garlic powder
    1 Tbsp. nutritional yeast (optional)   ¼ tsp. black pepper

Stir-fry until tofu starts to brown. Serve hot with toast or other grain.

Per Serving: Calories: 100, Protein 8 gm., Fat: 7 gm., Carbohydrates: 4 gm.

Zucchini Frittuta

Serves 4-6
Makes eight 5" frittatas

Saute lightly until crisp-tender:

3 Tbsp. olive oil
1 large onion, sliced thin
4 medium zucchini, sliced thin

¼ cup fresh parsley, chopped
3 fresh garlic cloves, pressed

Remove from heat.

In a separate bowl, mix together well:

¾ lb. tofu, blended
½ cup tofu, mashed
1½ tsp. salt

¾ cup flour
2 tsp. baking powder
1 Tbsp. soy sauce

Stir in the sauteed vegetables. Scoop out ½ cupfuls of mix on an oiled cookie sheet and flatten into circles. Or oil a large 10" cast iron skillet and fill with all of the mix. Bake for 15 minutes on one side, flip and bake 15 minutes more, or until golden brown. Serve with wide noodles and Tomato Sauce Topping, below.

Tomato Sauce Topping

Makes 2 cups sauce

Mix together in a saucepan:

1 (15 oz.) can tomato sauce
¼ cup water
1 Tbsp. olive oil
2 tsp. wine vinegar

½ tsp. garlic powder
½ tsp. salt
3 Tbsp. parsley, chopped fine

Simmer 20 minutes. Spread over frittatas.

Per Serving: Calories: 337, Protein: 13 gm., Fat: 19 gm., Carbohydrates: 32 gm.

Teriyaki Tofu

Serves 4-6

Cut into ½" slices:

1 lb. firm tofu

Make a marinade of:

2 Tbsp. soy sauce
1 Tbsp. fresh ginger root, minced
1 Tbsp. vinegar or lemon juice

1 tsp. honey or sweetener of your choice
1 clove garlic, minced
1 small onion, diced small

Pour marinade over the tofu slices in a glass or stainless steel pan and let marinate for 2 hours. Drain and reserve marinade. Dip the tofu slices in a mixture of:

¼ cup unbleached white flour
¼ tsp. black pepper

Brown the floured slices in:

2 Tbsp. oil

Add a little more oil, if necessary. Reduce heat, pour in reserved marinade and simmer 10 minutes.

Per Serving: Calories: 151, Protein: 8 gm., Fat: 10 gm., Carbohydrates: 10 gm.

Layered Casserole

Oil the baking dish with:
2 Tbsp. oil

Then dust the baking dish with:
2 Tbsp. flour

Blend each layer separately and spread evenly into the baking dish. Be careful not to mix the layers.

First Layer

Blend together in a food processor or blender:
1 lb. tofu
3 cups fresh spinach, chopped, cooked, and drained or
  1 (10 oz.) pkg. frozen spinach, cooked and drained
2 Tbsp. oil
1 tsp. salt

Second Layer

Blend together in a food processor or blender:
1 lb. tofu
2 Tbsp. oil
1 (7 oz.) jar pimentos, drained and chopped
1 Tbsp. lemon juice
1 tsp. salt

Third Layer

Blend together in a food processor or blender:
1½ lbs. tofu
2 Tbsp. oil
2 Tbsp. soy sauce
1 tsp. onion powder
1 tsp. salt
¼ tsp. garlic powder

Fold in:
1 cup fresh mushrooms, chopped in ¼" pieces

Bake at 350° F for 1 hour or until set. Let stand and cool a few minutes before serving. Can be served hot or cold

Per Serving: Calories: 193, Protein: 11 gm., Fat: 15 gm., Carbohydrates: 6 gm.

Layered Casserole

Chinese Sweet and Sour Balls

Serves 6
Makes sixteen 1½" balls

Preheat oven to 350° F.

Whip together:
1 Tbsp. peanut butter
1 Tbsp. soy sauce

Mash in a bowl:
1 lb. tofu

Mix into the mashed tofu:

½ cup whole wheat flour	**¼ cup fresh mushrooms, sliced**
the peanut butter-soy sauce mixture	**¼ cup fresh water chestnuts or celery, sliced**
½ cup green pepper, chopped in ¼" **pieces**	**4 green onions, sliced thin**

Form into sixteen 1½" balls, and arrange in an 8" x 8" pan spread with:
1 Tbsp. oil

Bake 20 minutes, then carefully turn each one over and bake 20 minutes more. Serve on rice with Sweet and Sour Sauce, below.

Sweet and Sour Sauce

Combine in a sauce pan over medium heat:

1 cup unsweetened pineapple juice	**2 Tbsp. soy sauce**
6 Tbsp. sweetener of your choice	**1½ Tbsp. arrowroot or cornstarch**
6 Tbsp. apple cider vinegar	**¼ tsp. garlic powder**

Whisk out all lumps, heat and stir constantly until thickened.

Per Serving: Calories: 211, Protein: 9 gm., Fat: 6 gm., Carbohydrates: 31 gm.

Sweet and Sour Tofu

Serves 4-6

Cut into small cubes (about ½"):
1 lb. firm tofu

Mix the cubes together with a mixture of:
½ cup cornstarch
    (or ¼ cup cornstarch and ¼ cup flour)
¼ cup vegetable bouillon or water
2 Tbsp. soy sauce

Deep-fry the cubes in oil heated to 365-368° F., being sure the cubes separate in the oil. Remove when golden brown (about 2-3 minutes). Drain and serve with Sweet and Sour Sauce, above, poured over.

Per Serving: Calories: 117, Protein: 7 gm., Fat: 4 gm., Carbohydrates: 14 gm.

Chinese Sweet and Sour Balls

Spring Rolls

Spring Rolls can be served as a main dish or an appetizer if made in a smaller size.

Have ready:
   12-15 ready-made eggroll wrappers
   either one of the fillings below

Be sure to have all ingredients ready before beginning to cook.

Spring Roll Filling No. 1

Cut into small strips or cubes:
   1 lb. firm tofu

Chop together in a food processor:
   2 cloves garlic
   1" cube fresh ginger root, peeled

Add and blend together with garlic and ginger:
   2 Tbsp. soy sauce
   2 Tbsp. mirin

Pour over the tofu pieces and let marinate while preparing vegetables:

2 scallions, chopped (¼ cup)	**1½ cups bok choy, chopped**
1 small bell pepper, sliced thin (1 cup)	**1 stalk celery, sliced thin diagonally**
3 cups cabbage, shredded	**1 cup mushrooms, sliced**

Heat wok and then add:
   1 Tbsp. oil

Immediately add scallions, pepper, mushrooms, and celery to the hot wok and stir-fry for 2 minutes. Add the cabbage, bok choy, and tofu, cover and steam 4 minutes, stir, cover and steam 4 minutes more. Stir together.

Spring Roll Filling No. 2

Freeze, thaw, and squeeze dry:
   1 lb. tofu

Cut tofu into small strips or cubes. Chop together in a food processor:
   1 clove garlic
   1" cube fresh garlic, peeled

Add and mix in:
   2 Tbsp. soy sauce
   1 Tbsp. rice vinegar

Pour over the tofu pieces and squeeze in evenly. Prepare vegetables below:

½ cup scallions, chopped	**3 cups bean sprouts**
1 cup snow peas, sliced (about ¼ lb.)	**6 oz. mushrooms, sliced**
1 cup bok choy leaves, chopped	**½ cup water chestnuts, chopped fine**

(Spring Rolls, continued on next page)

(Spring Rolls, continued)

Heat wok and then add:
1 Tbsp. oil

Immediately add scallions, snow peas and mushrooms to the hot wok and stir-fry for 2 minutes. Add tofu, water chestnuts, bok choy and bean sprouts. Cover and steam 4 minutes more. Stir together.

To prepare each Spring Roll, place ⅓-½ cup filling in the center of each wrapper. Bring one corner over and tuck around the filling, then fold the two side corners over on top. Roll it over, securing the top flap to the roll with a dab of water. Deep-fry two at a time in hot peanut or corn oil until golden brown. If the oil temperature is kept at 365-368° F, the rolls will brown without absorbing much oil at all. Do not let the oil smoke. Brown on both sides. Drain on absorbent paper and serve hot with Sweet and Sour Sauce, p. 76, or mustard or soy sauce.

Per Roll (No. 1): Calories: 141, Protein: 6 gm., Fat: 2 gm., Carbohydrates: 23 gm.

Per Roll (No. 2): Calories: 150, Protein: 7 gm., Fat: 2 gm., Carbohydrates: 24 gm.

Onion and Pepper Pie

Serves 6-8
Makes one 12" pizza pan
6-8 slices

Crust

Dissolve together in a measuring cup:
½ cup warm water
½ Tbsp. active dry yeast
½ Tbsp. honey

Measure into a food processor:
1½ cups unbleached white flour or whole wheat flour
¼ tsp. salt

Turn on food processor to mix dry ingredients. While it is running, pour in liquid and process until well kneaded. Transfer dough to a lightly oiled bowl, cover and let rise while preparing filling.

Preheat oven to 350° F.

Filling

Saute together until transparent:
1 Tbsp. olive oil
2 medium onions, sliced thin
1 medium green bell pepper, sliced thin
1 medium red bell pepper, sliced thin
1 clove garlic, minced

Blend in a food processor or blender until creamy:
1 lb. tofu
1 Tbsp. olive oil
½ tsp. salt
½ tsp. oregano
½ tsp. basil
¼ tsp. garlic powder or
1 clove garlic, minced

Roll the dough out on a board sprinkled with cornmeal to fit a 12" pizza pan. Spread the filling over the dough, as for pizza. Then spread the sauteed onion and pepper topping over the top. Bake about 25-30 minutes, or until crust is golden.

Per Slice: Calories: 188, Protein: 8 gm., Fat: 7 gm., Carbohydrates: 24 gm.

Korean Barbeque Tofu

Serves 6

Cut into ¼" slices:
1 ½ lbs. firm tofu

Marinate at least 2 hours (overnight is best) in a mixture of:
½ cup soy sauce
6 Tbsp. sugar or sweetener of your choice
2 tsp. dry mustard
4 cloves garlic, minced fine
or ½ tsp. garlic powder
2 tsp. onion powder

Brown on both sides in:
2 Tbsp. oil

Garnish with chopped green onion, mushrooms and/or snow peas and serve with rice. Can top with mushrooms and snow peas.

Per Serving: Calories: 187, Protein: 10 gm., Fat: 9 gm., Carbohydrates: 18 gm.

Marinating Korean Barbeque with the help of a baster

Tofu and Broccoli in Garlic Sauce

Serves 6

Cut into cubes:
1½ lbs. tofu

Marinate in:
¼ cup soy sauce

Carefully stir the marinating tofu occasionally while preparing the sauce.

Cut in half lengthwise, then into thin half-rings and set aside:
2 medium onions

Slice and set aside:
8 oz. fresh mushrooms

Crush and set aside:
1 bud garlic (medium size, 8-10 cloves)

Cut into large florets and set aside:
1 lb. broccoli

Dissolve together and set aside:
2 cups boiling water
2 cubes vegetable bouillon

Drain the tofu and reserve liquid. Brown tofu in a heavy skillet or wok on all sides in:
3 Tbsp. oil

Remove tofu when brown.

Add to the pan:
1 Tbsp. oil

Quickly fry the onions and mushrooms until soft.

Add and stir together:
the crushed garlic
the bouillon mixture
1 Tbsp. prepared Chinese mustard
3 Tbsp. honey
1 tsp. crushed red pepper (more or less to taste)
¼ tsp. ginger or
1 tsp. fresh ginger, peeled and grated

Add:
the tofu and reserved marinade

Simmer over medium heat for 1 minute, then add:
the cut broccoli

Simmer 3 minutes more. Turn off and set aside for 5 minutes. Serve over rice.

Per Serving: Calories: 247, Protein: 13 gm., Fat: 14 gm., Carbohydrates: 20 gm.

Tofu Knishes

These can be made smaller to be served as appetizers.

Have ready:
2 ½ cups cooked potatoes, peeled and mashed

Dough

Beat together:
1 cup potatoes, mashed
1 Tbsp. oil
1 tsp. salt

Add:
3 cups unbleached white flour or
1½ cups whole wheat and 1½ cups unbleached white
1 tsp. baking powder

Mix well, then mix in:
½ cup cold water

Knead into a smooth dough then let rest on a board, covered with a cloth, for ½ hour.

Filling

Saute until transparent:
2 Tbsp. oil
1 cup onions, chopped

Mix together with:

1½ cups potatoes, mashed	**1 tsp. salt**
1½ cups tofu, mashed	**½ tsp. garlic powder**
¼ cup fresh parsley, chopped	**¼ tsp. black pepper**

Cut the dough into 4 sections, then roll each section as thin as possible (about ¼₆" thick). Cut into 5" x 6" rectangles. Place 2 or 3 tablespoons of filling in the middle of each rectangle. Fold sides in first, then the ends.

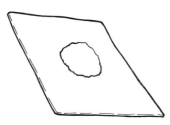

Place folded side down on an oiled cookie sheet. Bake at 350° F. for 25 minutes or until golden. Serve with horseradish or mustard.

Per Knish: Calories: 217, Protein: 7 gm., Fat: 6 gm., Carbohydrates: 29 gm.

Basic Fried Tofu

Serves 6-8
Makes 12-15 slices

There can be numerous variations to this recipe by substituting different herbs and flavorings. This is a basic recipe and you can take it from here to suit your own taste.

Cut into ¼"-½" slices:
1½ lbs. firm tofu

Heat in a skillet or griddle to medium heat:
1 Tbsp. oil

Arrange tofu slices in the pan and sprinkle with:
soy sauce or salt to taste
1-2 Tbsp. nutritional yeast
¼ tsp. garlic powder

When the tofu has browned on one side, flip it over and brown the other side. Serve hot as a main dish, in a sandwich or as a snack.

Variations: Try sprinkling the cooking slices with your favorite herb combination. Replace nutritional yeast by spreading slices with a little Vegemite or Marmite. Try dredging the slices in the flour mixture used for Oven-Fried Tofu, p. 90, and then frying.

Per Slice: Calories: 95, Protein: 8 gm., Fat: 6 gm., Carbohydrates: 3 gm.

Quiche

Serves 6-8
Makes one 8" pie

Preheat oven to 350° F.

Have ready:
1 unbaked 8" pie shell

Saute together:
2 Tbsp. oil
1 medium onion, chopped

When soft, add to:
1½ lbs. tofu, mashed   **1 Tbsp. dry mustard**
¼ cup nutritional yeast (optional)   **½ tsp. garlic powder**
3 Tbsp. fresh lemon juice   **¼ tsp. black pepper**
2 Tbsp. soy sauce

Mix well. Pour tofu mixture into pie shell. Bake for 45-60 minutes until set.

Variation: Cover the bottom of an unbaked pie shell with ¾ cup crumbled fried tempeh* which has been drained, or ½ cup imitation bacon bits, then fill with the tofu mixture and bake.

*Tempeh is a cultured soyfood made by incubating partially split soybeans. Tempeh is available in health or natural food stores.

Per Serving: Calories: 213, Protein: 9 gm., Fat: 15 gm., Carbohydrates: 13 gm.

Quiche with Tempeh

Jewish-Style Stuffed Cabbage Rolls

Serves 6

Have ready:
    1 cup cooked rice

Sauce

Mix and simmer in a large saucepan while preparing filling:

7 cups water	**6 Tbsp. sugar**
1 (6 oz.) can tomato paste	**2 Tbsp. lemon juice**
¼ cup raisins	**1 Tbsp. salt**

Filling

Saute together until limp:

3 Tbsp. oil	**1 clove garlic, chopped**
1 medium onion, chopped	

Turn off heat and mix in:

1½ lbs. tofu, mashed	**2 Tbsp. soy sauce**
1 cup cooked rice	**1 tsp. salt**

Wash 18 large cabbage leaves and put each leaf into boiling water for 1-2 minutes to soften. (It's all right to boil 3-4 at a time.) Drain and trim out the hard center core strip. Put 2-3 tablespoons of filling on each leaf, fold the sides in and roll up. You can use toothpicks to hold them together if needed. Carefully drop the rolls into simmering sauce — don't stir so they won't fall apart. Simmer 2-3 hours, not stirring, but pushing down on the top rolls occasionally. Can be served as they are or over mashed potatoes or rice.

Per Serving: Calories: 331, Protein: 14 gm., Fat: 12 gm., Carbohydrates: 41 gm.

Sloppy Joes

Serves 4-6

An All-American dish featuring tofu.

Saute until tender:

2 Tbsp. olive oil	**1 medium green pepper, chopped**
1 medium onion, chopped	**2 cloves garlic, minced**

Add to the pan:
    1 lb. tofu, crumbled
    2 Tbsp. soy sauce

Continue cooking and stirring until the tofu starts to brown. Then stir in:
    2 cups of your favorite tomato sauce
    1 Tbsp. chili powder
    ½ tsp. cumin powder

Serve hot over toasted burger buns.

Per Serving: Calories: 169, Protein: 10 gm., Fat: 9 gm., Carbohydrates: 14 gm.

Tofu Mushroom Roll

Filling

Saute together:
  1 Tbsp. oil
  8 oz. mushrooms, chopped

In another pan, saute until transparent:
  1 Tbsp. oil
  ¾ cup onions, chopped

Set aside ⅓ of the onions for the sauce. Then add the rest of the onions and the mushrooms to the mixture below:

1½ lbs. tofu, crumbled	**¾ tsp. thyme**
⅓ cup parsley, chopped	**¼ tsp. black pepper**
1 tsp. salt	

Dough

Mix together:

3 cups unbleached white flour	**1 tsp. salt**
4½ tsp. baking powder	

Pour in and mix:
  ½ cup oil

Pour in:
  1 scant cup cold water

Stir together to form a ball. Roll out ⅓" to ½" thick on a well-floured board into an oblong shape. Spread on the filling, being careful not to tear the dough. Roll it up lengthwise and seal the edge with water. Place on an oiled cookie sheet and cut slits in the top. Brush lightly with oil and bake at 400° F for 25-30 minutes until lightly browned.

Sauce

Lightly saute:
  1 Tbsp. oil   **8 oz. mushrooms, sliced**

In another pan, bubble together over low heat for 1 minute:
  2 Tbsp. oil
  ½ cup unbleached white flour

Stir in:

4 cups stock, vegetable bouillon	**1 Tbsp. soy sauce**
or soymilk	**¼ tsp. black pepper**

Cook until thickened, stirring any lumps out. Sauce will be thin. Stir in mushrooms and reserved sauteed onions. Pour over slices of the roll and serve.

Per Serving: Calories: 407, Protein: 12 gm., Fat: 23 gm., Carbohydrates: 37 gm.

Falafels

Have ready:
  8-10 purchased pita breads
  4 cups cooked chickpeas (garbanzo beans) and reserved cooking water

Blend together in a blender until creamy:
  4 cups chickpeas, drained
  1 cup chickpea cooking water
  3 cloves fresh garlic

Pour this into a mixing bowl and add:
  1 lb. tofu, mashed
  ⅓ cup soy sauce
  1 tsp. salt
  ¼ tsp. black pepper
  1 medium onion, chopped fine
  6 cups whole grain bread crumbs

Mix together until all ingredients are moist. Form 1½" balls and roll in unbleached white flour. Fry the balls in ½" oil at 350° F, turning each one until golden all around.

Cut pita breads in half and open pockets carefully. Pita breads can be warmed up in a moderate oven for a few minutes, but should remain soft. Put 2-3 balls in each pocket. Pour 1 tablespoon (more if you like) Tahini Sauce, below, over the balls and top with chopped tomatoes and lettuce.

Tahini Sauce

Chop fine in a food processor or blender:
  3 cloves fresh garlic

Add and blend until smooth:
  ½ cup tahini
  ¼ cup fresh lemon juice
  2 Tbsp. soy sauce

This may be served warmed up or cold. It will keep up to 2 weeks in the refrigerator and is also good on salads, fried tofu, or noodles.

Per Serving: Calories: 671, Protein: 29 gm., Fat: 23 gm., Carbohydrates: 99 gm.

Falafels

Vegetable Chow Yuk

Serves 6

In a wok or skillet, fry over medium low heat until all sides are browned:
¼ cup oil
1½ lbs. tofu, cut in 1½" cubes

Add:
1 medium onion, sliced   **6 green onions, cut in half lengthwise**
6 stalks celery, cut in 1" diagonal slices   **2 large bell peppers, sliced**

Cover and simmer for 5 minutes, stirring several times.

Mix together well:
½ cup water   **2 Tbsp. sugar or sweetener of your choice**
⅓ cup soy sauce   **½ tsp. garlic powder**

Pour over the tofu and vegetables. Cover and cook another 10 minutes.

In the last five minutes of cooking add and stir in:
2 cups fresh mung bean sprouts
½ lb. fresh mushrooms, sliced

Serve over hot rice.

Per Serving: Calories: 223, Protein: 12 gm., Fat: 14 gm., Carbohydrates: 15 gm.

Oven-Fried Tofu

Serves 8-10
Makes 16-20 pieces

Preheat oven to 350° F.

Cut into ¼"-½" slices:
2 lbs. firm tofu

Mix together in a bowl:
1¼ cups unbleached white flour   **2 tsp. garlic powder**
¼ cup nutritional yeast   **1 tsp. poultry seasoning**
2 Tbsp. onion powder   **½ tsp. black pepper**
1 Tbsp. parsley flakes

Pour into another bowl:
2 Tbsp. soy sauce

Spread a cookie sheet with:
2 Tbsp. oil

Using the one hand wet and one hand dry method, dip each slice first into the soy sauce on both sides, then dredge each slice in the flour mixture. Arrange the slices on the oiled cookie sheet and bake 20 minutes on the first side, then flip the slices and bake 15 minutes more or until each side is browned. Add a little more oil to the cookie sheet if necessary. Serve hot or cold, as a main dish, in sandwiches, or as a snack.

Per Slice: Calories: 170, Protein: 10 gm., Fat: 7 gm., Carbohydrates: 16 gm.

Tofu Turnovers

Makes 18 turnovers

These are good hot or cold, for lunchboxes or picnics, and can be frozen and reheated later.

Turnover Dough

Stir together in a large mixing bowl:
1½ cups potato water, warm
½ cup potatoes, mashed
2 Tbsp. oil
1 Tbsp. active dry yeast
1 Tbsp. sweetener of your choice

Let rise 10 minutes, then mix in gradually:
3½-4 cups whole wheat flour
3½-4 cups unbleached white flour
1 tsp. salt

Preheat oven to 425°F.

Knead the dough until smooth and not sticky. Divide into 18 balls about 2″ in diameter. On a floured board roll each one out into a 6″ circle or roll the dough out ⅛″ thick and cut into 6″ squares. Put 2-3 Tbsp. of Turnover Filling, below, in the center of each circle (or square) of rolled-out dough. Moisten the edges with water, fold over and seal by pressing the edges together with a fork.

Bake for about 15 minutes or until lightly browned. Be careful—they burn easily. Serve in a cloth-lined basket.

Turnover Filling

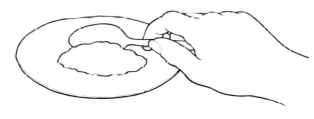

Saute together for about 10 minutes:
1 Tbsp. oil
3 cloves garlic, minced
3 medium carrots, sliced thin
3 stalks celery, sliced thin
1 medium onion, chopped
1 small green pepper, chopped
¾ cups snow peas, chopped or
  early peas (fresh or frozen)
1 tsp. salt

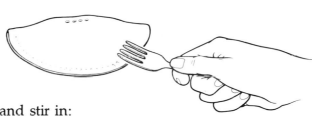

When vegetables are crisp tender, turn off heat and stir in:
1¼ lbs. tofu, mashed or chopped

Per Turnover: Calories: 241, Protein: 10 gm., Fat: 10 gm., Carbohydrates: 42 gm.

Taquitos

Crispy little tacos served with Avocado Sauce.

Have ready:
   24 corn tortillas

Freeze, thaw, squeeze dry, and tear into bite-size pieces:
   1½ lbs. tofu

Avocado Sauce

Peel and mash:
   2 ripe avocados

Stir in:
   1 cup green taco sauce (more if you like it hotter)
   1 tsp. garlic powder

Chill for one hour before serving.

Filling

Mix together:
   3 Tbsp. soy sauce
   2 Tbsp. peanut butter
   6 cloves garlic, pressed

Work this mixture into the bite-size tofu pieces, then mix in:
   1 cup onion, diced

Brown the whole mixture in:
   ¼ cup oil

Set aside.

Soften the tortillas by spreading them out on a cookie sheet and putting them in a preheated 350° F oven for about 2 minutes. The tortillas need to be soft and flexible to roll easily.

Lay 2-2½ tablespoons of filling across each tortilla and wrap the tortilla snugly around the filling. Insert a wooden toothpick through each end and in the middle of each one to keep it closed.

Taquitos can then be either pan-fried or oven-fried. Pan-fry 3 at a time in a heavy skillet with ¾″ oil heated to 350° F. When golden brown on one side, turn over to fry until golden brown on the other side. Then drain. To oven-fry, lay the rolled taquitos on an oiled cookie sheet, then put in a preheated 350° F oven for 8-10 minutes on each side or until crisp.

Remove the toothpicks and serve with Avocado Sauce. These can also be served with refried pinto beans, Spanish Rice and tossed green salad.

Per Serving: Calories: 477, Protein: 15 gm., Fat: 33 gm., Carbohydrates: 35 gm.

Won Ton

Serves 10-12

Won Ton may be deep-fried or boiled. This recipe maks 85-90 won ton, which uses up one package of won ton wrappers. Deep-fried as a main dish, this will serve about 10 to 12. If you are using them in soup you may want only 3 or 4 per serving. See p. 22 for Watercress Soup with Won Ton. The excess may be frozen and cooked later.

Have ready:
  1 pkg. won ton wrappers

Filling

Stir-fry together about 2 minutes in a wok or heavy skillet:
  1 Tbsp. oil
  1 Tbsp. ginger root, peeled and minced
  ¼ cup celery, chopped
  1 cup Chinese cabbage, chopped
  1 lb. tofu, crumbled fine
  1 Tbsp soy sauce
  1 cup fresh bean sprouts

There are many ways to fold a won ton. Your won ton package will show you some variations. One way is to start with a square and place one teaspoon of filling in the middle of the square. Wet the four edges of the square with dabs of water. Fold the wrapper in half diagonally to form a triangle and press the edges together. Fold it in half again, forming a long trapezoidal shape. Bring the longest ends together, then press and stick them together with a dab of water. This will form a pointed tail on the won ton.

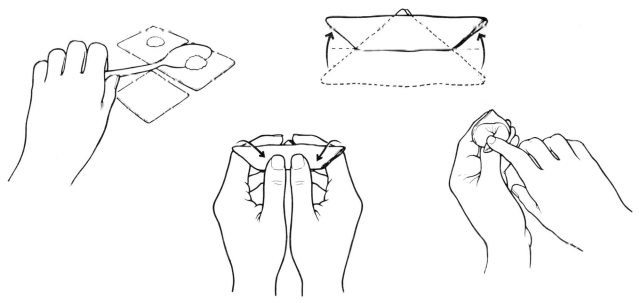

Another way is to cut your won ton wrappers into circles. This can be done several at a time with scissors or a sharp knife. Place one teaspoon of filling in the lower half of the circle. Fold the top half over and seal with a dab of water. Take the two corners of the resulting half-circle and bring them around to meet each other, pressing them together with a dab of water to make them stick.

Deep-fry won ton in 365-368° F. oil until golden brown. Drain and serve, or boil won ton in boiling water or soup for the last 5 minutes of cooking.

Per Serving: Calories: 157, Protein: 7 gm., Fat: 3 gm., Carbohydrates: 25 gm.

Stewart's Stew

Combine in a 5-quart saucepan and boil until vegetables are almost soft:

2½ qts. water	4 medium onions, chopped
5 medium potatoes, chopped	½ tsp. salt
6 carrots, chopped	

Meanwhile, cut into ¾" cubes and marinate for 15 minutes:

1 ½ lbs. tofu	½ cup soy sauce

Drain soy sauce into cooking vegetables.

Combine in a bag:

1 cup unbleached white flour	1 tsp. black pepper
1 tsp. salt	

Shake the bag to mix this up, then add the marinated tofu cubes to the bag and shake to coat the cubes.

Brown the breaded cubes in:
   ¼ cup oil

Be careful not to knock off the breading when turning the cubes. Add the browned cubes to the almost soft vegetables. Mix any leftover breading into a smooth paste with a little broth, then add to the stew. Continue boiling until vegetables are soft.

Per Serving: Calories: 337, Protein: 14 gm., Fat: 12 gm., Carbohydrates: 45 gm.

Tofu Paprika

Cut into ½" slices:
   1 lb. tofu

Lightly fry in:
   1 Tbsp. olive oil

While frying sprinkle with:
   ½ tsp. garlic powder (¼ tsp. on each side)

Remove tofu from pan and to the same pan add:

1 Tbsp. olive oil	½ tsp. salt
4 cups onions, thinly sliced	

When onions are lightly browned sprinkle with:
   1½ Tbsp. paprika

Cover with:
   1 cup vegetable bouillon, broth or water

Cover pan and simmer 10 minutes. Then stir in:
   1 recipe Tofu Sour Creme Dressing, p. 41

Return tofu to the pan, spooning sauce over, and heat through, but do not boil. Serve on rice, noodles, or mashed potatoes.

Per Serving: Calories: 255, Protein: 13 gm., Fat: 17 gm., Carbohydrates: 17 gm.

Eggplant Sandwiches

Preheat oven to 350° F.

Peel and cut into twelve to sixteen ½" slices:
1 medium eggplant

Spread out on paper towels and sprinkle with:
1 tsp. salt

Let these sit about 10 minutes, then wipe the salt off and dredge in a breading mixture of:

¼ cup unbleached white flour　　　**¼ tsp. garlic powder**
¼ cup cornmeal　　　**dash of black pepper**
½ tsp. oregano

Arrange the eggplant on a cookie sheet spread with:
1 Tbsp. olive oil

Bake about 8-10 minutes, then flip the eggplants over, adding to the cookie sheet:
1 Tbsp. olive oil

Bake 8-10 minutes more or until soft.

Filling

While the eggplant is baking, mix together:

1 lb. tofu, mashed well　　　**1 tsp. basil**
3 Tbsp. fresh lemon juice　　　**½ tsp. salt**
½ Tbsp. honey or sweetener of your　　　**½ tsp. garlic powder**
choice
½ Tbsp. onion powder

Spread half the slices with ¼-⅓ cup of filling, add a slice of ripe tomato and sprouts, then top with a second eggplant slice. Serve.

Per Serving: Calories: 130, Protein: 7 gm., Fat: 7 gm., Carbohydrates: 12 gm.

Side Dishes

Clockwise from top: Summer Vegetable Medley, Risotto Verde, and Penne Rigate with Sweet Red Pepper Sauce

SIDE DISHES

Risotto Verde

Serves 6-8

Preheat oven to 325° F.

Have ready:
   2 cups cooked rice, brown or white

Thaw and reserve liquid:
   **1 (10 oz.) pkg. chopped frozen spinach or
   2 cups chopped, blanched greens (spinach, kale or other favorites)**

Blend until smooth and creamy:
   **½ lb. tofu
   2 Tbsp. oil
   2 Tbsp. spinach juice (from thawing or blanching) or stock
   1 ½ tsp. salt**

Saute:
   **1 Tbsp. oil
   1 medium onion, finely chopped
   2 cloves garlic, minced**

Remove from heat and fold in:
   **the cooked rice
   ¼ tsp. freshly ground black pepper
   ⅛ tsp. nutmeg
   the thawed spinach
   the blended tofu mixture**

Bake in an oiled 1½ quart glass baking dish for 30 minutes.

Variation: Substitute ½ cup fresh chopped parsley for the spinach and leave out the nutmeg.

Per Serving: Calories: 149, Protein: 6 gm., Fat: 7 gm., Carbohydrates: 16 gm.

Java Tofu Pilaf

Serves 8-10

Cut into cubes:
1½ lbs. firm tofu

Mix together until smooth:
¼ cup soy sauce
2 Tbsp. peanut butter

Pour over the tofu cubes and mix together.

Brown the cubes in:
2 Tbsp. oil

In another skillet, saute:
1 Tbsp. oil
1 large onion, chopped

When the onion pieces become limp, add:

2½ Tbsp. fresh curry powder   **1 cup uncooked rice, brown or white**
½ tsp. coriander   **½ cup raisins**
½ tsp. cumin
1 tsp. salt

Mix all together and toast 5 minutes while stirring. Then pour in:
3½ cups boiling water or stock
the browned tofu

Mix, bring to a boil, stir, cover, turn heat to low and simmer 45 minutes for brown rice, 20 minutes for white rice. Serve.

Per Serving: Calories: 214, Protein: 12 gm., Fat: 9 gm., Carbohydrates: 25 gm.

Stuffed Baked Tomatoes

Serves 8-12

Wash 8 large or 12 small ripe tomatoes, then cut or scoop out a hollow on the stem end, leaving about ⅔-¾ of the tomato.

Stuffing

Saute together until soft:
2 Tbsp. oil
1 cup onion, diced
½ cup green pepper, diced

Preheat oven to 400° F.

Mix together in a bowl:

1 lb. tofu, mashed   **1 Tbsp. soy sauce**
¼ cup parsley, chopped fine   **¼ tsp. garlic powder**

Combine sauteed vegetables and tofu mixture. Stuff tomatoes and arrange in a 9" square oiled baking pan. Top with bread or cracker crumbs. Bake for 20 minutes. Serve hot or chilled.

Per Serving: Calories: 105, Protein: 5 gm., Fat: 6 gm., Carbohydrates: 9 gm.

POTATO Pancakes **NOT worTh making again**

Tofu Kartoffelkuchen

Serve 4-6
Makes eight 6" cakes

This also makes a good breakfast.

Mix together:

8 medium potatoes, grated
½ lb. tofu, blended
1 large onion, grated
¼ cup fresh parsley, chopped fine
3 Tbsp. unbleached white flour
1 tsp. salt
½ tsp. garlic powder
¼ tsp. black pepper

For each pancake, brush a 6″ skillet with oil and heat to medium heat. Spoon about ¾ cup of the potato mixture into the pan and flatten to ⅜″-½″ thick. Fry about 5-7 minutes on each side or until golden brown. Serve hot with applesauce on the side, or top with Tofu Sour Creme Dressing, p. 41.

Per Serving: Calories: 266, Protein: 8 gm., Fat: 11 gm., Carbohydrates: 36 gm.

Tofu Kartoffelkuchen

Walnut-Stuffed Zucchini

Serves 4-6

Preheat oven to 375° F.

Wash and trim the ends off:
4 small zucchini

Cut the zucchini in half lengthwise, scoop out the seed pulp and set aside. Parboil the shells for 1 minute and drain.

Saute together until transparent:
1 Tbsp. oil
⅓ cup onion, chopped

Beat together with an electric mixer:

¾ lb. tofu	**1 tsp. salt**
2 Tbsp. vinegar	**1 tsp. sweetener of your choice**
1 Tbsp. oil	**⅛ tsp. black pepper**

Chop the zucchini pulp and mix it together with sauteed onions and the tofu mixture.

Stir in:
⅓ cup walnuts, chopped

Heap onto shells. Sprinkle with paprika. Bake on an oiled sheet for 15-20 minutes.

Per Serving: Calories: 179, Protein: 9 gm., Fat: 13 gm., Carbohydrates: 9 gm.

Spinach Souffle

Serves 6-8

10 ☆

Preheat oven to 350° F.

Thaw:
1 (10 oz.) package frozen chopped spinach, reserving juice

Saute until limp:
3 Tbsp. oil
½ cup onion, chopped

Stir in:

3 Tbsp. unbleached white flour	**½ tsp. salt**
1 cup liquid (including spinach juice and water or soymilk)	**dash of freshly ground black pepper**
	dash of freshly ground nutmeg

Fold spinach into sauce.

Blend until smooth and creamy:

1 cup tofu	**½ tsp. salt**
2 Tbsp. fresh lemon juice or vinegar	**dash of freshly ground black pepper**
1 Tbsp. oil	

Fold into spinach and sauce. Bake in oiled 8″ round pan or 8″ square pan for 30 minutes.

Per Serving: Calories: 148, Protein: 7 gm., Fat: 10 gm., Carbohydrates: 7 gm.

Tofu Rice Ring

Serves 8-10
Makes one 5-6 cup ring

Have ready:
4 cups cooked rice, brown or white

Whip together:
¼ cup soy sauce
2 Tbsp. peanut butter
1 tsp. onion powder
¼ tsp. garlic powder

Pour this over:
1 lb. tofu, cut into ½″ cubes

Mix carefully until all cubes are coated.

Brown the cubes in:
2 Tbsp. oil

Saute together in another pan:
1 Tbsp. oil
1 large stalk celery, diced
4 green onions, cut in ½″ pieces

Preheat oven to 400° F.

Add sauteed vegetables and tofu to:
the cooked rice
½ cup black olives, pitted and sliced
¼ cup pimentos, chopped

Stir gently, then add:
½ cup blended tofu
⅛ tsp. black pepper

Stir gently again until just blended. Press firmly into a well-oiled 5-6 cup ring mold. Fit the ring mold inside another baking pan which has 1″ of water in the bottom, and bake for 20 minutes. Remove from the oven and let cool 5 minutes. Loosen the edges with a knife and turn out onto a platter. Serve with the center of the ring filled with steamed vegetables.

Per Serving: Calories: 301, Protein: 9 gm., Fat: 8 gm., Carbohydrates: 43 gm.

Summer Vegetable Medley

Serves 6-8

Fresh herbs and vegetables blend in a hearty summer vegetable harvest.

Stir fry over medium heat until onions and peppers start to soften:
   1 Tbsp. olive oil
   1 red onion, chopped
   1 red sweet bell pepper, chopped
   1 large clove garlic, minced
   1 lb. tofu, frozen, thawed, squeezed dry, and cubed

Add and continue to stir fry:
   1 small zucchini, sliced
   1 small yellow summer squash, sliced
   1 cup green beans, cut
   1 cup cut corn
   1 lb. plum tomatoes, peeled and chopped
   ¼ cup fresh basil leaves, packed and chopped
   3 Tbsp. fresh parsley, chopped
   1 tsp. salt
   ½ tsp. black pepper

Mix, cover and steam over low heat until vegetables are crisp tender and serve.

Per Serving: Calories: 111, Protein: 7 gm., Fat: 5 gm., Carbohydrates: 12 gm.

Chiliquiles

Cut or tear into bite-sized pieces:
2 dozen corn tortillas

Mix together and set aside:
½ lb. tofu, crumbled
1 (8 oz.) jar picante sauce
3 small cloves garlic, pressed

Heat in a large skillet or wok:
¼ cup oil

When hot (don't let it smoke) add:
the cut-up tortillas

Stir-fry over medium heat until the pieces are coated with oil.

Add:
1 medium onion, chopped

Stir-fry until the tortilla pieces are golden brown.

Sprinkle with:
1 tsp. salt

Add the tofu-picante sauce mixture to the pan and mix well. Cover and steam 2-3 minutes, until hot, and serve.

Per Serving: Calories: 334, Protein: 9 gm., Fat: 11 gm., Carbohydrates: 52 gm.

Chiliquiles

Tofu Fried Rice

Have ready:
4 cups cooled cooked rice, brown or white

Heat in a heavy skillet or wok:
1 Tbsp. oil
2 cloves garlic, crushed

Cook until garlic is light brown, then remove and discard the garlic.

Add and stir-fry for 1 minute:
¾ lb. tofu, diced

Add and stir in well:
1 Tbsp. soy sauce

Remove tofu from pan. Add to the pan:
1 Tbsp. oil
2 cloves garlic, minced

Stir-fry for 1 minute. Then add:
1½ cups onion, diced
1 cup celery, diced

Stir-fry for 2-3 minutes. Then add:
the cooked rice

Stir-fry until all mixed. Then add:
the diced and fried tofu
1½ cups fresh bean sprouts

Stir-fry 2 minutes. Then add:
1 Tbsp. soy sauce

Mix well. Serve hot, topped with chopped green onion.

Per Serving: Calories: 200, Protein: 8 gm., Fat: 6 gm., Carbohydrates: 29 gm.

Corn Pie

A South-of-the-Border casserole.

Preheat oven to 350° F.

Saute together until onions are transparent:
 1 Tbsp. oil
 1 medium onion, chopped

Add and fry for 5 minutes more:
 ¾ lb. tofu, crumbled
 1 tsp. chili powder
 ¼ tsp. black pepper
 2 dashes cayenne

Stir in:
 1 (17 oz.) can cut corn, drained or
 2 cups frozen whole kernel corn
 18 black olives, pitted and cut in half
 ½ cup water

Pour into an oiled 6½" x 10" pan.

Mix together in a bowl:
 ¾ cup corn meal
 ¼ cup unbleached white flour
 1 Tbsp. sweetener of your choice (if using a liquid sweetener, add to the wet
  ingredients)
 1 tsp. baking powder
 ½ tsp. salt
 ¼ tsp. baking soda

Pour into the flour mixture:
 ¾ cup soymilk
 2 Tbsp. oil
 (liquid sweetener)

Mix together until dry ingredients are moistened. Pour over the top of the corn and tofu mixture in the pan. Bake at 350° F. about 25 minutes until cornbread is golden.

Per Serving: Calories: 263, Protein: 9 gm., Fat: 9 gm., Carbohydrates: 28 gm.

Stuffed Bell Peppers Con Chili

Serves 6

Cut into 1" x ½" x ¼" pieces:
1 lb. firm tofu

Whip together:
3 Tbsp. soy sauce
3 Tbsp. peanut butter
2 tsp. onion powder
½ tsp. garlic powder

Pour over the tofu in a glass or stainless steel bowl. Mix together and let marinate for ½ hour.

Brown in:
2 Tbsp. oil

Wash and cut off the tops of:
6 large bell peppers

Remove stems, membranes and seeds, saving the tops. Parboil the shells in 1" boiling water for 5 minutes and set them up in an oiled baking dish.

Preheat oven to 400° F.

Saute:
2 Tbsp. oil
1 large onion, chopped
2 stalks celery, choppped
6 bell pepper tops, chopped

Add and mix together:
1 Tbsp. chili powder (more if you like)
2 cloves garlic, minced
1 tsp. cumin
½ tsp. oregano
1 cup tomato sauce
1½ cups cut corn
the browned tofu

Stuff the peppers and pour over all:
1 cup tomato sauce

Bake for about 25 minutes.

Variation: Cut the pepper in half lengthwise before parboiling and stuffing, and bake in a larger pan.

Per Serving: Calories: 272, Protein: 12 gm., Fat: 14 gm., Carbohydrates: 23 gm.

Penne Rigate with Sweet Red Pepper Sauce

Serves 6-8
Makes 3½ cups sauce

Boil in salted water to al-dente:
1 lb. penne rigate

Rinse and drain. Keep warm until served.

Saute until soft:
1 Tbsp. olive oil
2 medium carrots, sliced thin
(about 1 cup)
1 large onion, chopped
(about 1½ cups)

1 large sweet red pepper, chopped
(about 1½ cups)
1 large clove garlic, minced
3 Tbsp. fresh basil, minced

Cut in half:
1 (10.5 oz.) pkg. silken tofu

Blend half of the sauteed vegetables and half the silken tofu in a blender until creamy, them repeat for the other half. Return to the pan, heat, and add:
1 tsp. salt
¼ tsp. black pepper

Serve sauce when hot over warm pasta.

Per Serving: Calories: 307, Protein: 11 gm., Fat: 3 gm., Carbohydrates: 56 gm.

Sculloped Cabbage

Serves 4-6

Parboil for 5 minutes:
1 qt. cabbage, coarsely chopped
1 cup water

Saute:
2 Tbsp. oil
1 onion, chopped

Sprinkle over onion:
2 Tbsp. unbleached white flour
½ tsp. salt

Drain cabbage cooking water into onion and flour. Saute mixture and stir over how heat until thick.

Preheat oven to 350° F.

Blend or beat until smooth:
½ lb. tofu
1 tsp. salt
2 Tbsp. oil

2 Tbsp. vinegar
⅛ tsp. black pepper

Stir this mixture into the cabbage along with the sauteed onions. Pour all into 1½-pint baking dish, top with bread crumbs and sprinkle with paprika. Bake for 30 minutes.

Per Serving: Calories: 197, Protein: 6 gm., Fat: 13 gm., Carbohydrates: 12 gm.

Breads

Yeasted Bread and Rolls, Cinnamon Rolls, Flour Tortillas, Sesame Tofu Crackers, and Hush Puppies

BREADS

Pumpernickel Bread

Makes 2 loaves

This is a dark, moist bread.

Dissolve together and let rise until foamy (about 10 minutes):
- ¾ **cup warm water**
- **2 Tbsp. active dry yeast**
- **2 Tbsp. molasses**

Blend in a blender until smooth and creamy:
- ½ **lb. tofu**
- ¾ **cup warm water**

Stir the blended mixture into the foamy yeast mixture along with:
- **6 Tbsp. molasses**
- ¼ **cup oil**

Stir in:
- **3 cups dark rye flour**
- **3 cups whole wheat flour**
- **1 cup bread flour (high gluten)**
- **2 Tbsp. cocoa powder**

Turn the dough out on a floured board and knead until smooth. Place the kneaded dough in an oiled bowl, cover, and let rise about 2 hours in a warm place until about double in bulk. Punch down. Knead and shape into 2 round or oblong loaves. Let rise until almost double. Bake at 450° F. for 20 minutes. Reduce heat to 350° F. and bake about 30 minutes more or until the loaves sound hollow when tapped on the bottom. Brush oil on the top and let cool on a wire rack.

Per Slice (18 Slices Per Loaf): Calories: 220, Protein: 6 gm., Fat: 6 gm., Carbohydrates: 37 gm.

Yeasted Bread or Rolls

Makes 2 loaves or 36 rolls

Boil until soft:
3 medium potatoes

Set aside.

Dissolve together in a large mixing bowl:
1 cup warm potato water
2 Tbsp. active dry yeast
1 Tbsp. honey

Let rise 10 minutes.

Blend in a blender until smooth and creamy:
½ lb. tofu
1½ cups cooked potatoes, mashed and cooled
1 cup warm water

Stir contents of the blender into the foaming yeast mixture.

Stir in:
4 cups unbleached white flour
1 Tbsp. salt
½ cup oil

Beat well. Let rise in a warm place for 20 minutes.

Stir down and add:
3-4 cups unbleached white flour

Knead into a smooth, soft dough. Form into 2 loaves or about 36 rolls. Put in oiled pans or oiled cookie sheets. Let rise about 20 minutes, until almost double in bulk. Preheat oven to 375° F. Bake for 40 minutes for loaves or 20 minutes for rolls.

Variation: For Cinnamon Rolls, knead the dough into a smooth ball. Divide in half and roll out each half on a well-floured board into a large rectangle ³⁄₁₆″ to ¼″ thick. Sprinkle and spread half of the filling, below, over all of the dough. Roll up each rectangle of dough, jelly-roll style. Slice into 1″ rounds and place about 1″ apart on oiled cookie sheets. Sprinkle the rest of the filling on top of the rolls. Let rise about 10 minutes. Bake for about 20 minutes.

Cinnamon Roll Filling

Mix together in a bowl:

1 cup unbleached white flour   **1 tsp. salt**
1 cup sugar   **½ cup oil**
1 Tbsp. cinnamon

Stir in:
½ cup raisins

Per Slice (18 Slices Per Loaf): Calories: 138, Protein: 3 gm., Fat: 4 gm., Carbohydrates: 21 gm.

Per Cinnamon Roll: Calories: 206, Protein: 4 gm., Fat: 7 gm., Carbohydrates: 31 gm.

Danish

Makes 24 danish

Dough

Dissolve together:
1 (1 Tbsp.) pkg. active dry yeast   **1 cup warm water**
1 Tbsp. sweetener of your choice

Let stand 5 minutes, then mix in:
2 cups unbleached white flour   **3 Tbsp. sweetener of your choice**

Beat well and let rise until doubled.

Dissolve together, then mix into the flour and yeast mixture with your hands:
½ cup oil   **1 tsp. salt**
¼ cup sweetener of your choice

Add to make a kneadable dough:
about 1½ cups more unbleached white flour
(2½ cups if you used a liquid sweetener)

Knead until smooth and soft, but not sticky. Let rise until double again.

Tofu Filling

Blend in a blender until smooth and creamy:
½ cup water   **1 cup soft tofu, crumbled**
¼ cup oil

Pour this into a small saucepan and whisk in:
¼ cup fresh lemon juice   **½ tsp. salt**
½ cup sweetener of your choice   **2 Tbsp. unbleached white flour**

Cook over medium heat, stirring constantly until thickened. Remove from heat and cool before filling the danish dough. Preheat oven to 350° F. Roll the dough out to ⅛″ thick. Brush with oil and cut into 4″ x 4″ squares. Place 1 scant tablespoon of filling in the center of each square. You can add about 1 scant tablespoon of cherry or blueberry pie filling on top of the Tofu Filling. Fold two opposite corners of the dough toward the middle and pinch together. Take the remaining unfolded corners and curl them in toward the filling. Let rise 5 minutes. Place on a well-oiled cookie sheet. Leave ½″ to 1″ space between each danish. Bake for about 15 minutes or until light golden brown. Brush with oil for last 3 minutes of baking.

Variation: For Prune Danish, place 1 scant tablespoon Prune Filling, below, in the center of each square (instead of tofu filling.) Bring all four corners toward the middle and pinch together. Place on a well-oiled sheet and follow the baking instructions, above.

Prune Filling

Cook covered until tender and then put through a food mill to make puree:
1 (16 oz.) box prunes, pitted   **2 cups water**

Stir in:
1½ Tbsp. fresh lemon juice

Per Danish (With Tofu Filling): Calories: 161, Protein: 3 gm., Fat: 7 gm., Carbohydrates: 21 gm.

Per Danish (With Prune Filling): Calories: 165, Protein: 2 gm., Fat: 5 gm., Carbohydrates: 29 gm.

Rum Rolls

Filled rolls for breakfast or brunch.

Dissolve together:
½ cup warm water
1 Tbsp. active dry yeast
¼ cup sweetener of your choice

Let foam together in a warm place 5-10 minutes. Then mix in:
1 cup unbleached white flour

Let sit 5-10 minutes more, then mix in:
¼ cup oil
4-5 cups more unbleached white flour
1 tsp. salt

Stir until blended. Cover and let rise in a warm place until double. While dough is rising, prepare filling below. Punch dough down and divide in half. Roll each half into a rectangle ⅜″ thick. Spread with filling, roll up each rectangle and cut into 1″ thick slices. Put each slice into an oiled muffin cup. Cover and let rise until almost double. Bake for 15-20 minutes. Cool and brush with frosting, below. These rolls freeze well.

Filling

Beat together:
¾ cup brown sugar
½ lb. tofu, crumbled or mashed
2 Tbsp. oil
2 tsp. rum flavoring
½ tsp. salt

Stir in:
1 cup raisins, plumped in hot water and drained

Frosting

Beat together and brush over the rolls:
1 cup powdered sugar
2-3 Tbsp. hot water
1 tsp. rum flavoring

Per Roll: Calories: 200, Protein: 4 gm., Fat: 4 gm., Carbohydrates: 38 gm.

English Muffins

Mix in a large bowl and let sit 10 minutes:
   1 (1 Tbsp.) pkg. active dry yeast
   1 cup warm water
   2 Tbsp. sweetener of your choice

Blend in a blender until smooth and creamy:
   ½ lb. tofu
   ½ cup warm water
   1 tsp. salt

Pour this into the foaming yeast mixture along with:
   3 Tbsp. oil

Stir in until smooth:
   3½ cups unbleached white flour

Mix in to make a soft dough:
   1-1½ cups unbleached white flour

Knead on a floured board for about 5 minutes. Let the dough rise in an oiled bowl until almost double in bulk. Punch down the dough and divide in half. Roll each half out on a generous amount of cornmeal to ½″ thick. Cut dough in 3″ circles. Let rise 10 minutes. Cook on a dry griddle or cast iron skillet over low heat for about 5-8 minutes on each side or until golden brown.

Per Muffin: Calories: 168, Protein: 5 gm., Fat: 3 gm., Carbohydrates: 28 gm.

Flour Tortillas

Mix together in a medium mixing bowl:
   4 cups unbleached white flour
   1 tsp. salt

Blend in a blender until smooth:
   ½ lb. soft tofu
   1¼ cups water
   2 Tbsp. oil

Make a well in the flour mixture, add liquid and stir well. Knead into a smooth dough on a well floured board. Divide into 14-16 balls about 1½″ in diameter. On a floured board roll each ball out into an 8″ circle.

Cook on a hot, dry griddle for a few seconds on each side until bubbly and brown-flecked on each side. Tortillas are best served right off the griddle, but can also be stacked inside a damp towel and reheated later.

Per Tortilla: Calories: 134, Protein: 4 gm., Fat: 3 gm., Carbohydrates: 23 gm.

Blueberry Sally Lunn

Makes one 9" x 13" pan
12-16 pieces

A mildly sweet and fruity breakfast bread.

Preheat oven to 350° F.

Mix together in a bowl:
2 cups unbleached white flour
2½ tsp. baking powder

Blend together in a food processor or blender:
⅓ cup oil
½ cup honey
1 (10.5 oz.) pkg. silken tofu
½ cup water
1 tsp. vanilla

Add the dry ingredients to the food processor and pulse just until mixed.

Then fold in:
1 cup blueberries, fresh or frozen

Pour into an oiled 9" x 13" pan and bake for about 25 minutes. Serve hot.

Per Serving: Calories: 156, Protein: 3 gm., Fat: 6 gm., Carbohydrates: 24 gm.

Tofu French Toast

Makes 8 slices

A breakfast treat.

Blend in a blender until smooth and creamy:
1½ cups tofu
1½ tsp. cinnamon
¼ cup honey
1 tsp. salt
½ cup water
2 Tbsp. oil

Pour into a shallow bowl.

Dip slices of day-old whole grain or home-made bread in batter, then fry in a hot skillet with 1 tablespoon oil for each side. Brown well on both sides. Serve with honey or maple syrup.

Per Slice: Calories: 243, Protein: 10 gm., Fat: 15 gm., Carbohydrates: 11 gm.

Buckwheat Cakes

Makes eighteen 4" cakes

Mix together in a large mixing bowl:

1 cup buckwheat flour
1 cup unbleached white flour
2 tsp. baking powder

1 tsp. baking soda
½ tsp. salt

Blend together in a blender:

½ lb. soft tofu
2½ cups water
2 Tbsp. oil
2 Tbsp. honey

Make a well in the dry ingredients and pour in the wet ones. Stir until batter is smooth. It will look somewhat gooey.

Heat the griddle over medium-high heat. Oil lightly and pour about ¼ cup batter for each cake. When the tops of the cakes bubble and look dry, flip them over and brown the other side. Serve hot with honey, syrup or jam.

Per Pancake: Calories: 79, Protein: 2 gm., Fat: 3 gm., Carbohydrates: 11 gm.

Tofu Pancakes

Serves 4-6
Makes eighteen 4" pancakes

Mix thoroughly together:

2 cups unbleached white flour
½ cup cornmeal
4½ tsp. baking powder

1 tsp. salt
¼ cup sugar (or add ¼ cup honey to wet ingredients)

Gently stir in with only a few strokes:

3 cups soymilk
2 Tbsp. oil

Batter will be lumpy.

Fold in gently:

½ lb. tofu, drained and well crumbled

Let batter sit while griddle heats. Fry on a lightly oiled griddle and serve.

Per Pancake: Calories: 78, Protein: 3 gm., Fat: 4 gm., Carbohydrates: 11 gm.

Banana Bread

Makes 1 loaf

Preheat oven to 350° F.

Blend in a blender until smooth and creamy:
¾ cup tofu

Pour into a mixing bowl and beat in:
1 cup sugar   **1 tsp. vanilla**
¼ cup oil   **1 cup ripe bananas, mashed**

Mix together in another bowl:
2 cups unbleached white flour   **½ tsp. baking soda**
½ tsp. baking powder   **¼ tsp. salt**

Beat everything together, then fold in:
¾ cup walnut pieces

Pour into an oiled loaf pan. Bake for about 1 hour.

Per Slice (12 Slices Per Loaf): Calories: 262, Protein: 5 gm., Fat: 10 gm., Carbohydrates: 39 gm.

Hush Puppies

Makes twenty-four 1" x 3" pups

Mix together in a 3 quart bowl:
2 cups unbleached white flour   **1¼ tsp. salt**
2 cups cornmeal   **4 tsp. baking powder**

Blend in a blender until smooth:
½ lb. soft tofu
1½ cups water

Stir in:
¼ cup oil

Make a well in the middle of the dry ingredients and add liquid. Stir until all ingredients are moistened.

Add:
½ cup onion, finely chopped

Mix all together. Use 2 tablespoons of dough to form a log or ball and fry them in 1" oil at 350° F. Brown on both sides. Serve as they are or with mustard.

Variation: For Sweet Hush Puppies, omit the onion and add 2 tablespoons sweetener of your choice to liquid ingredients. Serve hot with honey or jam.

Per Pup: Calories: 126, Protein: 3 gm., Fat: 5 gm., Carbohydrates: 16 gm.

Cornmeal Muffins

Makes 12 muffins

Preheat oven to 425° F.

Mix together:
2 cups cornmeal
2 cups unbleached white flour
1½ tsp. salt

2 tsp. baking powder
½ tsp. baking soda

Blend a blender until smooth and creamy:
½ lb. soft tofu
1½ cups water

Pour into bowl and then stir in:
¼ cup oil
3 Tbsp. honey or molasses

Stir the wet ingredients into the dry ingredients until moistened. Fill oiled muffin tins three-quarters full. Bake for 15-20 minutes or until golden brown.

Per Muffin: Calories: 232, Protein: 6 gm., Fat: 7 gm., Carbohydrates: 36 gm.

Sesame Tofu Crackers

Makes 50 crackers

Preheat oven to 400° F.

Mix together in a bowl:
3 cups unbleached white flour or
whole wheat flour
1 tsp. salt
3 Tbsp. sesame seeds
1 tsp. baking powder

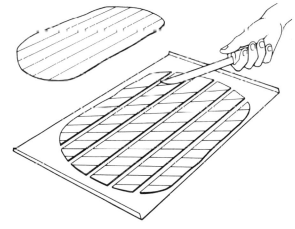

In a blender, blend until smooth and creamy:
½ lb. tofu
½ cup oil
¼ cup water

Make a well in the middle of the dry ingredients and pour in the blended mix. Mix well. Add up to ¼ cup water if necessary to make a soft dough.

Roll out on a lightly floured board to ¹⁄₁₆″ thick and cut in 3″ x 14″ strips. Place on a cookie sheet and cut the strips diagonally.

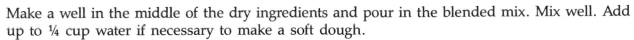

Bake for 12-15 minutes or until golden brown. Watch them carefully so they don't burn. These will keep well if stored in an airtight container.

Per Cracker: Calories: 55, Protein: 1 gm., Fat: 3 gm., Carbohydrates: 6 gm.

Noodles

Serves 4-6

Blend in a blender until smooth and creamy:
- **½ lb. tofu**
- **2 Tbsp. oil**
- **½ tsp. salt**

Pour this into:
- **1¾ cups unbleached white flour**

Mix and knead until smooth and soft (about 10 minutes). Put through a noodle machine or roll out by hand and cut. Let dry 15 minutes. Boil in salted water about 5 minutes.

Per Serving: Calories: 254, Protein: 8 gm., Fat: 7 gm., Carbohydrates: 36 gm.

Spinach Noodles

Serves 4-6

Blend in a blender until smooth and creamy:
- **1 cup fresh spinach, washed, dried, and chopped**
- **½ cup tofu**
- **2 Tbsp. oil**
- **½ tsp. salt**

Pour this into:
- **2 cups unbleached white flour**

Mix and knead until smooth and soft (10 minutes). Put though a noodle machine or roll out by hand and cut. Let dry 15 minutes. Boil in salted water about 5 minutes.

Per Serving: Calories: 265, Protein: 8 gm., Fat: 7 gm., Carbohydrates: 40 gm.

Noodles and Spinach Noodles

Cookies and Bars

Clockwise starting from Soymilk: Oatmeal, Peanut Butter and Soft Molasses Cookies, Jam Dot Cookies, Chocolate Brownies, Chocolate Chip Bars, Date-Nut Bars, and Carob Honey Brownies

COOKIES AND BARS

Jam Dot Cookies

Makes 48 cookies

Preheat oven to 350° F.

Have ready:
  ¼ cup any flavor of jam

Blend in a blender until creamy:
  ½ lb. tofu
  ½ cup walnuts

Pour the blended mixture into a bowl and mix in:

½ cup oil	**1 tsp. salt**
2 cups sugar	**1 tsp. baking soda**
1 tsp. vanilla	**4 cups unbleached white flour**

Mix well by hand or electric mixer. Roll into 1 ½" balls and place them 2" apart on oiled cookie sheets. Press thumb in the middle of each ball, leaving a depression. Bake for 10 minutes. Remove sheets from oven and drop ¼ teaspoon of jam in each depression. Bake 2-3 minutes more. Store when cool with wax paper between layers.

Per Cookie: Calories: 110, Protein: 2 gm., Fat: 3 gm., Carbohydrates: 17 gm.

Carob Honey Brownies

Makes one 9" square pan

Preheat oven to 350° F.

Blend in a blender until creamy:

½ lb. tofu	**1 Tbsp. vanilla**
1 cup honey	**⅔ cup carob powder**
½ cup oil	**¾ cup water**

In a separate bowl, mix:
  1 ¾ cups unbleached flour
  ¾ tsp. baking soda
  1 tsp. baking powder

Add wet ingredients and mix well.

Fold in:
  ½ cup walnuts, chopped

Oil and flour a 9" square pan. Spread batter evenly. Bake for 25-30 minutes. Cool and cut into 12 brownies.

Per Brownie: Calories: 293, Protein: 4 gm., Fat: 13 gm., Carbohydrates: 47 gm.

Brownies

Makes one 10" square pan

Preheat oven to 350° F.

Whisk together in a saucepan, leaving no lumps:
⅓ cup unbleached white flour
⅔ cup water

Whip in:
½ lb. tofu, blended until smooth and creamy

Stir constantly over low heat until thickened. Cool completely.

To the cooled mixture, add:
2 cups sugar
1 tsp. salt
1 tsp. vanilla

Beat well.

In another bowl mix together:
¾ cup cocoa powder
½ cup oil

Add to the other ingredients and stir well.

Mix together:
1½ cups unbleached white flour
1 scant tsp. baking powder

Add this to the mixture above and stir until there are no lumps. Bake in a well-oiled and floured 10" square pan for 25 minutes or until a knife inserted in the middle comes out clean. Cut into 12 brownies.

For cake-like brownies, increase baking powder to 2 teaspoons and bake for 20 minutes.

Per Brownie: Calories: 383, Protein: 6 gm., Fat: 12 gm., Carbohydrates: 64 gm.

Soft Molasses Cookies

Makes 36 cookies

Preheat oven to 350° F.

Blend in a blender until smooth and creamy:
1 cup molasses or sorghum   **½ lb. tofu, mashed**
1 cup oil   **½ cup brown sugar**

Mix together dry ingredients:
3½-4 cups unbleached white flour
½ tsp. baking soda
¼ tsp. salt

Mix together wet and dry ingredients until well blended. Drop by spoonfuls onto an oiled cookie sheet. Bake for about 10 minutes. Store in tightly covered container to preserve moisture.

Per Cookie: Calories: 144, Protein: 2 gm., Fat: 7 gm., Carbohydrates: 9 gm.

Oatmeal Cookies

Makes 48 cookies

Preheat oven to 350° F.

Blend in a blender until smooth and creamy:
   ¾ cup soft tofu

Pour into a bowl and mix together with:
   1 cup oil
   1½ cups honey
   1 Tbsp. vanilla

In another bowl mix together:

4 cups rolled oats	1 tsp. baking soda
2½ cups unbleached white flour	½ tsp. salt
1 tsp. baking powder	

Mix the dry ingredients into the wet along with:
   ½ cup walnuts, broken
   ½ cup raisins

Drop by heaping tablespoonfuls onto oiled cookie sheets and bake for 15 minutes.

Per Cookie: Calories: 121, Protein: 2 gm., Fat: 4 gm., Carbohydrates: 20 gm.

Gingerbread Cut-Out Cookies

Makes 10 very large cookies

Blend in a food processor or mixer until creamy:

1 cup sorghum or molasses	¼ cup oil
1 cup tofu (½ lb.)	

Mix together in a bowl:

3½ cups unbleached white flour	½ tsp. salt
3 tsp. ginger	¼ tsp. allspice
1 tsp. baking soda	⅛ tsp. cloves
1 tsp. cinnamon	⅛ tsp. nutmeg

Pour the dry ingredients into the wet and pulse or mix until blended. Do not over-mix or the cookies will be tough. If you are mixing with a spoon, you may have to use your hands to mix the last part. Chill the dough overnight.

Preheat oven to 350° F.

Roll out the dough ⅛″ to ¼″ thick. Cut in desired shapes and bake on oiled cookie sheets for about 8 minutes.

Per Very Large Cookie: Calories: 275, Protein: 6 gm., Fat: 7 gm, Carbohydrates: 47 gm.

Peanut Butter Cookies

Makes 48 cookies

Preheat oven to 350° F.

Mix together:
3 cups unbleached white flour
1 tsp. baking soda
½ tsp. salt

In another bowl mix together:

½ cup oil
1 cup peanut butter
1 cup brown sugar

½ cup honey
½ cup tofu, blended
1 tsp. vanilla

Mix the dry ingredients into the wet ones. Form the dough into 1″ balls. Arrange the balls on a cookie sheet about 3″ apart. Press with a fork (that has been dipped in cold water) in a criss-cross design, then bake for 10-12 minutes.

Per Cookie: Calories: 112, Protein: 2 gm., Fat: 5 gm., Carbohydrates: 12 gm.

Tofu Fudge Chews

Makes 48 cookies

These cookies keep well in an airtight container. They have a moist, chewy center with a crisp, sugar-coated outside.

Blend in a blender until smooth:
½ lb. tofu
½ cup oil

Pour into a medium mixing bowl. Add:

1½ cups sugar
½ cup cocoa powder

1 Tbsp. vanilla (optional)
1 Tbsp. water or soymilk

Stir well. Mix separately;
3 cups unbleached white flour
1 tsp. baking soda
1 tsp. salt

Add to wet ingredients. Mix well. The dough should be fairly stiff. Roll into 1½″ balls. In a saucer put:
½ cup sugar

Roll the formed balls in the sugar until they are coated. Place on a lightly oiled cookie sheet 1″ apart. Bake for 12-15 minutes at 350° F. Cool on a wire rack.

Per Cookie: Calories: 92, Protein: 1 gm., Fat: 3 gm., Carbohydrates: 15 gm.

Date-Nut Bars

Makes one 9" x 13" pan

Preheat oven to 375° F.

Cook over low heat until thickened:
2 (8 oz.) pkgs. dates, pitted and chopped (2½ cups)
2½ cups water

Set aside while preparing the following cookie mix.

Beat together in a medium mixing bowl:
½ cup tofu, soft and mashed   **¾ cup honey**
½ cup oil   **1 tsp. salt**

Add and beat in:
2 cups unbleached white flour   **1 cup nuts, chopped**
1½ cups oats, quick-cooking   **(almonds, pecans, walnuts, or peanuts)**
¾ tsp. baking soda

Press three-quarters of the dough into an oiled 9" x 13" pan. Spread date filling evenly over dough. Crumble remaining dough over dates. Bake for 15-20 minutes. Cool and cut into 24 bars.

Note: For a crunchier cookie, substitute ¾ cup brown sugar for the honey.

Per Bar: Calories: 487, Protein: 6 gm., Fat: 8 gm., Carbohydrates: 105 gm.

Banana-Chocolate Chip Cookies

Makes about 24 cookies

Preheat oven to 350° F.

Blend in a food processor or blender until smooth:
½ cup oil   **2 small ripe bananas**
½ cup brown sugar   **1 tsp. vanilla**
½ cup tofu

Pulse 4 times to mix in:
2 cups whole wheat pastry flour   **½ tsp. baking soda**
½ tsp. baking powder

Fold in:
1 cup chocolate chips
½ cup walnuts, chopped (optional)

Drop by tablespoons onto cookie sheets. Bake about 15 to 20 minutes, or until browned on the bottom.

Per Cookie: Calories: 138, Protein: 2 gm., Fat: 6 gm., Carbohydrates: 17 gm.

Pecan-Coconut Bars

Makes one 9" square pan

Preheat oven to 350° F.

Beat with an electric beater:

½ cup tofu, mashed	2 Tbsp. lemon juice
⅓ cup oil	1 tsp. salt

Beat in:

1 cup brown sugar, packed	⅔ cup dried coconut
1 ½ cups unbleached white flour	1 tsp. vanilla
½ cup oatmeal	1 tsp. baking powder

Fold in:

½ cup pecan pieces

Pour into an oiled pan. Bake for 25-30 minutes. Cool, and cut into 12 bars.

Per Bar: Calories: 268, Protein: 4 gm., Fat: 13 gm, Carbohydrates: 34 gm.

Chocolate Chip Bars

Makes one 9" x 13" pan

Preheat oven to 350° F.

Cream together:

¾ cup white sugar
¾ cup brown sugar
1 cup oil

Blend in a blender:

⅓ cup tofu, mashed
2 Tbsp. water
1 tsp. vanilla

Add to the sugar and oil. In a bowl, mix together:

3½ cups unbleached white flour	½ tsp. baking soda
1½ tsp. baking powder	½ tsp. salt

Mix wet and dry ingredients together, then fold in:

1 cup chocolate chips

Press into a 9" x 13" pan and bake 10-12 minutes, until lightly browned. Cool and cut into 24 bars.

Per Bar: Calories: 229, Protein: 3 gm., Fat: 10 gm., Carbohydrates: 33 gm.

Desserts

Clockwise from top left: Cheesecake, Gingerbread Cut-Out Cookies, Carrot Cake, Pumpkin Pie, Creamy Coconut Pie, Black Bottom Pie, and Gingerbread Cut-Out Cookies
Center: Strawberry Pudding and Apricot Whip

DESSERTS

Orange-Vanilla "Custard"

Serves 8-10
Makes one 9½" deep-dish pie pan

If you are using a blender, be sure to read "Blending Tofu" on p. 7, before blending more than ½ lb. at a time.

Preheat oven to 400° F.

Blend in a food processor or blender until smooth and creamy:
2 lbs. tofu, crumbled
⅔ cup frozen orange juice concentrate, thawed
2 Tbsp. oil
1 tsp. vanilla
½ tsp. salt

In a bowl, mix together:
1 cup sugar
½ cup unbleached white flour
1 tsp. baking powder
¼ tsp. baking soda

Add this mixture slowly to the mixture in the food processor or blender, blending until smooth.

Pour the mixture into the well-oiled and floured pan. Bake for about 30 minutes. Serve hot or cold. Slice with a sharp wet knife. The texture becomes denser as it cools.

Per Serving: Calories: 240, Protein: 9 gm., Fat: 7 gm., Carbohydrates: 36 gm.

Banana Dessert

Serves 6-8

Quick and easy. If using a blender, read "Blending Tofu" on p. 7 before blending more than ½ lb. at a time. If you use plantanos instead of bananas, this will make twice as many servings.

Preheat oven to 350° F.

Blend in a food processor or blender until smooth and creamy:
1 lb. tofu   **2 Tbsp. oil**
1¼ cups sugar   **1½ tsp. cinnamon**
3 Tbsp. lemon juice or vinegar   **½ tsp. salt**

Set this mixture aside. Cut in half lengthwise:
6 firm bananas or an equal amount of plantanos

Fry the banana halves over medium heat until brown in:
2 Tbsp. oil

Arrange half the bananas flat side up and cover with half the blended tofu mixture. Arrange the rest of the bananas on top and cover with the rest of the blended tofu mixture. Bake for 20-30 minutes. Serve hot.

Per Serving: Calories: 271, Protein: 6 gm., Fat: 3 gm., Carbohydrates: 59 gm.

Plum Noodle Kugel

Preheat oven to 350° F.

Mix together:

- **1 lb. flat noodles, cooked and drained**
- **1½ cups sugar**
- **1½ lbs. tofu, mashed**
- **1½ cups applesauce**
- **1½ tsp. cinnamon**
- **3 lbs. plums (canned) pitted and quartered**

Spread this mixture evenly in an oiled 9″ x 13″ pan.

Mix together:

- **¾ cup chopped nuts**
- **¾ cup fine whole grain bread crumbs**

Crumble this mixture evenly over the top, then drizzle with:

- **3 Tbsp. oil**

Bake for 45 minutes. Serve hot or cold with Sweet and Creamy Topping, p. 145.

Per Serving: Calories: 364, Protein: 9 gm., Fat: 9 gm., Carbohydrates: 61 gm.

Pumpkin Pie

A holiday favorite.

Preheat oven to 350° F.

Have ready:

- **1 unbaked 9″ pastry crust**

Blend in a food processor or blender until smooth and creamy:

- **¾ lb. tofu**
- **1 (16 oz.) can pumpkin (2 cups)**
- **1 cup light brown sugar**
- **2 Tbsp. oil**
- **2 Tbsp. molasses**
- **1½ tsp. cinnamon**
- **1 tsp. salt**
- **¾ tsp. ginger**
- **½ tsp. nutmeg**

Pour this mixture into the unbaked pastry shell. Bake for 1 hour, or until small cracks start to appear in the filling. Chill and serve with Sweet and Creamy Topping, p. 145.

Per Serving: Calories: 320, Protein: 6 gm., Fat: 13 gm., Carbohydrates: 49 gm.

Creamy Coconut Pie

Serves 8-10
Makes one 9" pie

Quick and easy.

Preheat oven to 350° F.

Have ready:
1 prebaked graham cracker pie shell

Blend in a food processor or blender until smooth and creamy:
1½ lbs. tofu
1½ cups confectioners' sugar
¼ cup oil
2 tsp. vanilla
½ tsp. salt

Fold in:
1-2 cups coconut, dried and sweetened

Pour into the pie shell. Bake for 15 minutes.

Sprinkle on top:
¼ cup coconut

Bake another 5 minutes or until the filling looks firm and set. Serve chilled.

Per Serving: Calories: 441, Protein: 9 gm., Fat: 19 gm., Carbohydrates: 52 gm.

Black Bottom Pie

Serves 8-10
Makes one 9" pie

Have ready:
1½ cups Sweet and Creamy Topping, p. 145, chilled
one 9" baked graham cracker crust or pastry shell, cooled

Blend in a food processor or blender until smooth and creamy:
1 lb. tofu
1½ cups confectioners' sugar
6 Tbsp. cocoa
¼ cup oil
1 tsp. vanilla
¾ tsp. soy sauce

Cover the bottom of a thoroughly cooled graham cracker pie crust with:
½ oz. unsweetened baking chocolate, grated or shaved

Then pour in the filling. Chill overnight. Top with Sweet and Creamy Topping, p. 145, and garnish with unsweetened chocolate shavings.

Per Serving: Calories: 479, Protein: 10 gm., Fat: 22 gm., Carbohydrates: 56 gm.

Frozen Peanut Butter Pie

Serves 8-10
Makes one 9" pie

A deliciously creamy, frozen dessert that is very easy to make.

Have ready:
one 9" baked pie shell

Blend in a food processor or blender until smooth and creamy:
1 lb. tofu	**¼ cup oil**
¾ cup peanut butter	**1 tsp. vanilla**
½ cup honey	**⅛ tsp. salt**

Pour into the baked pie shell. Decorate with semi-sweet chocolate shavings or curls. Freeze. Let thaw for about 10 minutes before serving.

Per Serving: Calories: 339, Protein: 10 gm., Fat: 18 gm., Carbohydrates: 27 gm.

Cannoli

Makes 8-9

A melt-in-your-mouth Sicilian pastry.

Have ready:
cannoli molds or a piece of 1" x 6" wooden dowel
(a clean piece of an unpointed broom stick would work)

Cannoli Shell Dough

Combine:
1 scant cup unbleached white flour	**¼ tsp. cinnamon (optional)**
2 Tbsp. sugar	**¼ tsp. salt**

Stir in to form a ball:
3½ Tbsp. water	**1 Tbsp. oil**

Knead into a smooth ball. Roll the dough out into a 15" x 15" square. Cut into 5" squares. Place mold or dowel in the center of square, fold very loosely (for easy removal) around the mold and seal lengthwise with a dab of water along edge. Deep fry in oil at 350° F. until light brown (about 2 minutes) and drain on absorbent paper. Remove the mold or dowel and start the next shell. Be careful not to let the oil smoke. Let all the shells cool before filling.

Cannoli Filling

Blend in a food processor or blender until smooth and creamy:
1 lb. soft tofu	**2 cups confectioners' sugar**
⅓ cup ǀ 2 Tbsp. oil	**1 tsp. vanilla extract**
1 Tbsp. lemon juice	**¼ tsp. almond extract (to your taste)**

Pour into a bowl and fold in:
½ cup mini chocolate chips

Chill the filling at least 2 hours. Stuff the shells with filling and serve immediately.

Per Serving: Calories: 480, Protein: 6 gm., Fat: 28 gm., Carbohydrates: 5 gm.

TOFU CHEESECAKES

Tofu Cheesecakes can be made with a variety of flavors and sweeteners. A medium firm tofu is good for chessecake. Be sure to read "Blending Tofu" on p. 7. If your tofu is very soft, it is best to put it between two towels, then put a weight on it for a while to remove excess moisture. When a Tofu Cheesecake is done baking, it will be slightly risen on the edges with small cracks appearing on the suface. The middle will not have risen, but will be springy to slight pressure from a finger. It will have a dry, firm look.

Cheesecake

Serves 10-12
Makes one 10" pie or 10" spring form pan

Quick and easy.

Preheat oven to 375° F.

Have ready:
1 baked graham cracker pie shell

Blend in a food processor or blender until smooth and creamy:
2 lbs. tofu	**½ cup honey**
1 cup sugar	**2 tsp. vanilla**
¼ cup fresh lemon juice	**pinch of salt**
¼ cup oil	

Pour this mixture into the baked crust. Bake for about 40 minutes or until small cracks start to appear on the surface. Serve well chilled, topped with fresh or frozen fruit.

Per Serving: Calories: 384, Protein: 9 gm., Fat: 13 gm, Carbohydrates: 56 gm.

Honey Cheesecake

Serves 10-12
Makes one 9" pie

Quick and easy.

Preheat oven to 350° F.

Have ready:
1 baked 9" graham cracker pie shell

Blend in a food processor or blender until smooth and creamy:
2 lbs. tofu	**¼ cup lemon juice**
1 cup honey	**2 tsp. vanilla**
¼ cup oil	**pinch of salt**

Pour this mixture into the baked pie shell and bake for about 1 hour, or until small cracks start to appear on the surface.

Serve well-chilled, topped with fresh or frozen fruit.

Per Serving: Calories: 364, Protein: 9 gm., Fat: 13, Carbohydrates: 51 gm.

Chocolate Cheesecake with Black Cherry topping
and Honey Cheesecake

Chocolate Cheesecake

Serves 10-12
Makes one 10" spring form pan

This recipe is pictured on p. 138.

Have ready in the bottom of a 10" spring form pan:
1 prebaked graham cracker crust

Drain between 2 towels with a breadboard weight on top for about 20 minutes:
2½ lbs. tofu

Blend the drained tofu, ½ pound at a time, until smooth and creamy. With each ½ pound in the blender, add:
½ cup sugar (2½ cups in all)

Pour all the blended tofu and sugar in a bowl. (The tofu and sugar can be blended all at once in a food processor.)

Preheat oven to 350° F.

Melt in a double boiler and add to the blended tofu mixture:
6 (1 oz.) squares semi-sweet chocolate

Mix together well along with:
2 tsp. vanilla   **pinch of salt**
1 tsp. almond extract   **½ cup more sugar**

Pour this mixture into the prebaked crust and bake for about 40 minutes. When chilled, top with fresh fruit glaze.

Per Serving: Calories: 381, Protein: 9 gm., Fat: 22 gm., Carbohydrates: 23 gm.

Maple Tofu Cheesecake

Serves 4-6
Makes one 8" pie

Quick and easy.

Have ready:
Your favorite recipe for an 8" pie shell

Preheat oven to 350° F.

Blend in a food processor or blender until smooth and creamy:
1½ lbs. tofu
3 Tbsp. oil
1⅓ cups maple syrup
pinch of salt

Pour this mixture into unbaked pie shell. Bake for 1 hour or until set. Serve cold, topped with maple syrup and pecans, or Sweet and Creamy Topping, p. 145.

Per Serving: Calories: 520, Protein: 12 gm., Fat: 23 gm., Carbohydrates: 69 gm.

Lemon Pudding, Chocolate Pudding, and Vanilla Pudding

TOFU PUDDINGS

Tofu Puddings are a creamy, delicious, high-protein treat. A medium or Japanese-style tofu is good for making puddings. Read "Blending Tofu" on p. 7 before starting. Puddings can be served chilled in individual serving dishes or chilled in a baked pie shell. For a creamy, frozen dessert, pour any flavor pudding into a baked pie shell and then freeze. Let the pie thaw for 15 minutes before slicing and serving.

For calorie-counters, these puddings can be made without oil (you may need to add some other liquid) and the amount of sweetener decreased. Banana-Date and Orange-Date Puddings use only the fruit for sweeteners.

Vanilla Pudding

Makes 4 cups

Blend in a food processor or blender until smooth and creamy:

1½ lbs. soft tofu
¼ cup oil
1 cup sugar, ⅞ cup honey,
   or sweetener of your choice

1 Tbsp. vanilla
pinch of salt

Pour into individual serving dishes or baked pie shell. Chill until set and serve.

Per ½ Cup Serving: Calories: 217, Protein: 7 gm., Fat: 11 gm., Carbohydrates: 26 gm.

Orange-Date Pudding

Makes 5 cups

This pudding is sweetened by orange juice and dates.

Blend in a food processor or blender until smooth and creamy:
1½ lbs. soft tofu	¼ cup oil
¾ cup pitted dates	1 tsp. vanilla
½ cup frozen orange juice concentrate	pinch of salt

Pour into individual serving dishes or baked pie shell. Chill until firm and serve.

Per ½ Cup Serving: Calories: 155, Protein: 6 gm., Fat: 8 gm., Carbohydrates: 15 gm.

Orange Pudding

Makes 4½ cups

Blend in a food processor or blender until smooth and creamy:
1½ lbs. soft tofu	1 tsp. vanilla
¼ cup oil	⅛ tsp. salt
¾ cup sugar	¾ cup frozen orange juice concentrate

Pour into individual serving dishes or a baked pie shell. Chill until firm and serve.

Per ½ Cup Serving: Calories: 212, Protein: 6 gm., Fat. 9 gm., Carbohydrates: 28 gm.

Chocolate Pudding

Makes 4 cups

Blend in a food processor or blender until smooth and creamy:
1½ lbs. soft tofu	¼ cup oil
1¼ cups sugar	1½ tsp. vanilla
⅓ cup cocoa	¼ tsp. salt or soy sauce

Pour into individual serving dishes or baked pie shell. Chill until firm and serve.

Per ½ Cup Serving: Calories: 254, Protein: 8 gm., Fat: 11 gm., Carbohydrates: 33 gm.

Banana Pudding

Makes 3 cups

Blend in a food processor or blender until smooth and creamy:
1 lb. tofu	2 tsp. vanilla
¼ cup oil	2 bananas, ripe
¼ tsp. salt	½ cup sugar

Pour into individual serving dishes or baked pie shell. Chill until set and serve.

Per ½ Cup Serving: Calories: 240, Protein: 6 gm., Fat: 12 gm., Carbohydrates: 29 gm.

Banana-Date Pudding

Makes 3 cups

This pudding is sweetened by fruit.

Blend in a food processor or blender until smooth and creamy:

1 lb. tofu	**1 tsp. lemon juice**
¼ cup oil	**¼ tsp. salt**
2 tsp. vanilla	**½ cup pitted dates, chopped**
2 Tbsp. soymilk	**2 bananas, ripe**

Pour into individual serving dishes or baked pie shell. Chill until set and serve.

Per ½ Cup Serving: Calories: 251, Protein: 7 gm., Fat: 13 gm., Carbohydrates: 32 gm.

Banana Honey Pudding

Makes 4 cups

Blend in a food processor or blender until smooth and creamy:

1½ lbs. tofu	**1 Tbsp. vanilla**
½ cup honey	**¼ tsp. salt**
¼ cup oil	**3 medium bananas, ripe**

Pour into individual serving dishes or baked pie shell. Chill until set and serve.

Per ½ Cup Serving: Calories: 228, Protein: 7 gm., Fat: 11 gm., Carbohydrates: 29 gm.

Carob Honey Pudding

Makes 3½ cups

Blend in a food processor or blender until smooth and creamy:

1½ lbs. tofu	**1 Tbsp. vanilla**
⅔ cup carob powder	**2 tsp. lemon juice**
½ cup honey	**pinch of salt**
¼ cup oil	

Pour into individual serving dishes or baked pie shell. Chill until set and serve.

Per ½ Cup Serving: Calories: 238, Protein: 8 gm., Fat: 12 gm., Carbohydrates: 32 gm.

Apricot Whip

Makes 3½ cups

Steam over boiling water until soft:
   18-20 dried apricot halves (about ½ cup)

Blend soft apricots in a food processor or blender until smooth and creamy with:

1 lb. tofu	**⅛ tsp. salt**
½ cup honey or sugar	**¼ cup oil**

Pour into individual serving dishes or baked pie shell. Chill until set and serve.

Per ½ Cup Serving: Calories: 194, Protein: 5 gm., Fat: 11 gm., Carbohydrates: 22 gm.

Lemon Pudding

Makes 3 cups

Blend in a food processor or blender until smooth and creamy:

- **1 lb. tofu**
- **¼ cup oil**
- **⅔ cup sugar**
- **⅛ tsp. salt**
- **6 Tbsp. lemon juice**
- **½ tsp. vanilla**

Pour into individual serving dishes or baked pie shell. Chill until set and serve.

Per ½ cup serving: Calories: 218, Protein: 6 gm., Fat: 12 gm., Carbohydrates: 24 gm.

Strawberry Pudding

Makes 3½ cups

Blend in a food processor or blender until smooth and creamy:

- **1½ cups tofu**
- **1½ cups fresh ripe strawberries**
- **½ cup sugar or sweetener of your choice**
- **¼ cup oil**
- **1 Tbsp. lemon juice**
- **1 tsp. vanilla**
- **pinch of salt**

Pour into individual serving dishes or baked pie shell, then chill overnight.

Per ½ Cup Serving: Calories: 206, Protein: 8 gm., Fat: 12 gm., Carbohydrates: 18 gm.

Carob Honey Pudding, Strawberry Pudding, and Orange Pudding

TOFU TOPPINGS

Serve Tofu Toppings as you would whipped cream. Use only very fresh, softer tofu for these toppings and blend them very creamy. Read "Blending Tofu" on pg. 7. If you are trying to reduce calories, you can omit the oil from these recipes, which will only slightly change their texture. Serve Tofu Toppings well chilled.

Sweet and Creamy Topping
Makes 1½ cups

Blend in a food processor or blender until smooth and creamy:
- **½ lb. tofu**
- **¼ cup oil**
- **¼ cup confectioners' sugar**
- **1 tsp. vanilla**
- **½ tsp. lemon juice**
- **⅛ tsp. salt**

Chill and serve as you would whipped cream.

Per ¼ Cup Serving: Calories: 129, Protein: 3 gm., Fat: 10 gm., Carbohydrates: 7 gm.

Sweet and Creamy Topping with Honey
Makes 1½ cups

Blend in a food processor or blender until smooth and creamy:
- **½ lb. soft tofu**
- **¼ cup oil**
- **2 Tbsp. honey**
- **½ Tbsp. lemon juice**
- **½ tsp. vanilla**
- **¼ tsp. salt**

Chill and serve as you would whipped cream.

Per ¼ Cup Serving: Calories: 129, Protein: 3 gm., Fat: 11 gm., Carbohydrates: 7 gm.

TOFU CAKES

Adding tofu to cakes makes a moist cake along with giving a higher protein level. Softer tofu is best for cakes. For successful Tofu Cakes, follow the directions exactly. Put your cake in a preheated oven immediately after mixing the wet and dry ingredients together. Be sure to bake at exactly the temperature specified. Try to avoid baking Tofu Cakes on damp or rainy days.

Blueberry Lemon Cake

Serves 12-14
Makes one 10" tube or bundt pan

Preheat oven to 350° F.

Blend together in a food processor:
  ½ **lb. tofu**
  ¾ **cup water**
  ½ **cup fresh lemon juice**
  ½ **cup oil**

Mix together in a bowl:
  2½ **cups unbleached white flour**
  1¼ **cups sugar**
  1½ **tsp. baking soda**
  ½ **tsp. salt**

Pour flour mixture into the food processor and pulse just until blended. Gently fold in:
  1 cup blueberries, fresh or frozen

Pour into an oiled tube or bundt pan and bake about 45 to 50 minutes. Let the cake cool about 10 minutes, then turn it out of the pan onto a rack. When the cake is cooled, move it onto a serving platter and glaze with Lemon Glaze, below.

Lemon Glaze

Mix together:
  1½ **cups confectioners' sugar**
  2 **Tbsp. fresh lemon juice**

Pour over the top of the cooled cake.

Per Serving: Calories: 300, Protein: 4 gm., Fat: 9 gm., Carbohydrates: 51 gm.

Blueberry Lemon Cake and Carrot Cake

Creme-Filled Crumb Cake

Serves 12-14
Makes one 10" tube or bundt cake

Preheat oven to 350° F.

Use three separate bowls to make the three separate layers.

First layer

Mix together until crumbly:

1 cup unbleached white flour	**2 Tbsp. oil**
½ cup brown sugar	**½ tsp. salt**
½ cup walnuts, chopped	

Press this mixture into the bottom and sides of the pan.

Second layer

Blend in a food processor or blender until smooth and creamy:

1 lb. tofu	**2 Tbsp. arrowroot or cornstarch**
½ cup sugar	**1 Tbsp. vanilla**
2 Tbsp. oil	**½ tsp. salt**

Spread on top of the first layer.

Third layer

Blend in a food processor or blender until smooth and creamy:

½ lb. tofu	**¼ cup oil**
1 cup water	**3 Tbsp. lemon juice**
1 cup sugar	

Add and pulse in the food processor or stir in until just blended with no lumps:

2 cups unbleached white flour	**½ tsp. baking soda**
½ cup walnuts, chopped	**½ tsp. cinnamon**
2 tsp. baking powder	**½ tsp. salt**

Pour and spread this over the second layer, being careful not to stir the second and third layers together. Bake for 40-45 minutes. Let cool 5-10 minutes, then loosen the edges and turn out onto a rack to cool. When cool, transfer to a serving plate and slice.

Per Serving: Calories: 389, Protein: 9 gm., Fat: 16 gm., Carbohydrates: 54 gm.

Shortcake

Serves 6
Makes twelve 3" cakes

Preheat oven to 400° F.

Mix together in a bowl:
2 cups unbleached white flour   **2 tsp. baking powder**
⅓ cup sugar   **½ tsp. salt**

Cut in:
⅓ cup oil

Set aside.

Blend in a blender until smooth and creamy:
½ cup tofu
¾ cup water

Mix well with dry ingredients, stirring until the dough is smooth. Roll out ¼" thick. Cut with a 3" biscuit cutter. Place half the circles on an oiled cookie sheet.

Oil the top of each with:
1 tsp. oil

Place another circle on top of each oiled one. Bake for 15 minutes.

When shortcakes are cool, split each one apart and spoon in Sweet and Creamy Topping, p. 145, and then spoon on fresh fruit. Put on the top half of the shortcake and spoon on more topping and fruit.

Per Serving: Calories: 441, Protein: 6 gm., Fat: 23 gm., Carbohydrates: 44 gm.

Chocolate Pudding Cake

Serves 9
Makes one 9" square pan

Preheat oven to 350° F.

Stir together:
1¼ cups unbleached white flour   **1½ tsp. baking powder**
¾ cup sugar   **¼ tsp. salt**
¼ cup cocoa powder

Beat in:
¾ cup tofu, crumbled small   **3 Tbsp. oil**
⅔ cup water   **½ cup walnuts or pecans**
1 tsp. vanilla

Pour into oiled pan.

Mix together:
2 Tbsp. cocoa powder
1 cup sugar

Sprinkle over the top of the batter in the pan, then pour on 1 cup boiling water. Bake for 45 minutes. Serve hot or cold.

Per Serving: Calories: 285, Protein: 5 gm., Fat: 11 gm., Carbohydrates: 45 gm.

Carrot Cake

Serves 16
Makes one 9" x 13" pan or
one 9" spring form tube pan

This recipe is pictured on p. 147.

Preheat oven to 350° F.

Mix together dry ingredients:
  3 cups unbleached white flour
  2 tsp. baking powder
  1 tsp. baking soda
  1 tsp. cinnamon
  1 tsp. salt

Mix well in a separate bowl:
  ½ lb. tofu, blended until smooth
  1 lb. carrots, grated (4½-5 cups)
  ¾ cup oil
  2 cups light brown sugar
  1 Tbsp. vanilla
  ¼ cup orange juice concentrate

Add dry ingredients to the wet ones. Stir until all dry parts are moistened.

Fold in:
  ¾ cup walnuts, chopped
  ¾ cup raisins

Oil and flour pan. Bake for 45 minutes. When cool, top with Creamy Glaze Topping, below.

Creamy Glaze Topping

Blend in a blender until smooth and creamy:
  ½ lb. tofu
  1 Tbsp. oil
  1 Tbsp. lemon juice
  3 Tbsp. honey
  ¼ tsp. salt

Per Serving: Calories: 388, Protein: 6 gm., Fat: 16 gm., Carbohydrates: 57 gm.

Peach-Strawberry Upside Down Cake

Serves 16
Makes one 9" x 13" pan

Preheat oven to 350° F.

Mix together in the bottom of a 9" x 13" pan:
¼ cup oil
¾ cup brown sugar

Pat it out evenly over the bottom of the pan, then arrange on top:
1 (1 lb.) can sliced peaches, drained
about 20 strawberries

Mix together in a bowl:
2½ cups unbleached flour
2½ tsp. baking powder
pinch of salt

Blend together in a food processor:
⅓ cup oil
1⅓ cups sugar
1 (10.5 oz.) pkg. silken tofu
½ cup water
1 tsp. vanilla

Pour the flour mixture into the food processor and process just until blended (about 10 seconds). Pour and spread over the fruit evenly. Bake about 30 minutes or until golden.

Per Serving: Calories: 264, Protein: 3 gm., Fat: 9 gm., Carbohydrates: 43 gm

TOFU ICE CREAM

Tofu Ice Cream has its own unique creamy texture. Serve it as you would any ice cream—in a bowl, on pie a la mode, or in a banana split. Try it also between graham crackers and refrozen as a sandwich, or spread in a prebaked pie shell and frozen. For a lower calorie and fat content, these ice creams can be made without oil.

Strawberry Tofu Ice Cream

Makes 12½ cups

Blend in a blender in four equal parts until smooth and creamy:

2 lbs. soft tofu
1 cup soymilk
2 cups sugar
1⅓ cups oil
¼ cup fresh lemon juice

2 (20 oz.) pkgs. frozen unsweetened
  strawberries
2 Tbsp. vanilla
¼ tsp. salt

Freeze in a home hand-operated or electric ice cream maker and serve.

Per ½ Cup Serving: Calories: 204, Protein: 3 gm., Fat: 14 gm., Carbohydrates: 20 gm.

Pineapple Tofu Ice Cream

Makes 13 cups

Blend in a blender in four equal parts until smooth and creamy:

2 lbs. soft tofu
1⅓ cups soymilk
1⅓ cups oil
2 cups sugar
¼ cup fresh lemon juice
2 Tbsp. vanilla

2 (20 oz.) cans unsweetened crushed
  pineapple with syrup (reserving ⅔ cup
  drained pineapple to stir in before
  freezing)
¼ tsp. salt

Stir in the reserved ⅔ cup drained pineapple. Freeze in a home hand-operated or electric ice cream maker and serve.

Per ½ Cup Serving: Calories: 213, Protein: 3 gm., Fat: 13 gm., Carbohydrates: 23 gm.

Carob Honey Tofu Ice Cream

Makes 9 cups

Blend in a blender in four equal parts until smooth and creamy:

2 lbs. tofu
2 cups soymilk
1 cup oil
1 cup honey

6 Tbsp. carob
3 Tbsp. vanilla
¼ tsp. salt

Freeze in a home hand-operated or electric ice cream maker and serve.

Per ½ Cup Serving: Calories: 223, Protein: 5 gm., Fat: 15 gm., Carbohydrates: 20 gm.

Pineapple Tofu Ice Cream, Chocolate Tofu Ice Cream, and Strawberry Tofu Ice Cream

Chocolate Tofu Ice Cream

Makes 10 cups

Blend in a blender in four equal parts until smooth and creamy:

2 lbs. soft tofu   **½ cup cocoa powder**
2 cups soymilk   **2 Tbsp. vanilla**
1 cup oil   **¼ tsp. salt**
2 cups sugar

Freeze in a home hand-operated or electric ice cream maker and serve.

Per ½ Cup Serving: Calories: 224, Protein: 5 gm., Fat: 14 gm., Carbohydrates: 23 gm.

Banana Honey Tofu Ice Cream

Makes 8 cups

Blend in a blender in four equal parts until smooth and creamy:

1 lb. tofu   **⅔ cup honey**
2 cups soymilk   **3 Tbsp. vanilla**
¾ cup oil   **¼ tsp. salt**
5 bananas, ripe

Freeze in a home hand-operated or electric ice cream maker and serve.

Per ½ Cup Serving: Calories: 209, Protein: 4 gm., Fat: 13 gm., Carbohydrates: 23 gm.

Peach Tofu Ice Cream

Makes 13 cups

Marinate together in the refrigerator for one hour:

8 medium peaches, peeled and chopped (about one quart)
the juice of 2 lemons
1 cup sugar

Combine with:

3 cups soymilk   **4 Tbsp. vanilla**
1½ lbs. tofu   **½ tsp. salt**
1¼ cups sugar

Blend in a blender in four equal parts until smooth and creamy. Freeze in a home hand-operated or electric ice cream maker and serve.

Per ½ Cup Serving: Calories: 137, Protein: 3 gm., Fat: 2 gm., Carbohydrates: 18 gm.

MAKING TOFU AT HOME

Making tofu at home is easy to do. It takes some time and organization and provides satisfying results. You will need:

- dried soybeans
- a food processor, blender, hand grain mill, or meat grinder
- a 3 or 4 gallon heavy pot or double boiler
- another large pot or bowl
- a large wire whisk
- a 2 to 3 foot square piece of nylon mesh or several layers of cheesecloth
- a large wooden paddle or spoon
- a colander
- a ladle
- a ½ gallon jug (to fill with water for a weight)

You will also need a curding agent. Any one of the following will do:

- vinegar (5%)
- lemon juice
- Epsom salts
- nigari

We used vinegar for curding the tofu in these pictures. Vinegar and lemon juice are probably the most widely available curding agents. Epsom salts can be found in drugstores, and nigari can be found in health food stores. Nigari is made by removing the salt and water from sea water, leaving the remaining minerals in crystal form. Different curding agents give different subtle flavors, texture, and yield in amount of curds. Too much solidifier will give the tofu a strong flavor that is not appetizing. Tofu should have a subtle, fresh flavor.

Home-made Tofu

Preparing the soybeans

Five cups of soybeans makes about 3½ to 4 lbs. of tofu. Start by rinsing and then soaking 5 cups of whole soybeans in 15 cups cold water overnight, or at least 8 to 10 hours. You can quick-soak your beans by pouring 15 cups of boiling water over the rinsed soybeans and letting them soak for 2 to 4 hours. Soybeans will double in size and be free of wrinkles when they are finished soaking. If you split one in half, it will have a flat surface inside, rather than a concave surface. Be sure to keep the soaking beans in a cool place or under refrigeration if the water is very hot so they won't sour. Soured beans will make thinner milk and therefore less yield.

After the soybeans have been soaked, rinse them in a colander. Now they are ready for grinding. You can use a food processor, grinding 2 cups of soaked soybeans at a time into slightly gritty or sandy paste. The grinding can also be done in a meat grinder, using the finer grind. If it is ground too smoothly it will be hard to strain and the resulting milk will have a pulpy texture. If it is not ground finely enough, it will not give a good yield.

Cooking the Soymilk

Using a large wire whisk, whip the soybean paste into about 2 gallons of rapidly boiling water (3 cups boiling water to every cup of soaked beans). Bring it back to a boil, turn down to medium heat, and let it cook at a low boil for 15 to 20 minutes, stirring occasionally. Watch the pot carefully, because soymilk can foam up and boil over quickly. Keep a cup of cold water next to the pot, to pour in if it starts to foam up quickly.

If you cook on an electric stove, you may have to remove the pot from the burner to adjust the heat if it starts to boil over.

Adding the soybean paste to boiling water

Cooking the soymilk

Blender Method

The grinding can also be done in a blender. For every cup of soaked soybeans, add 3 cups of water to the blender. The water can be either hot or cold. Blend this at high speed into a fine slurry (about one minute), then pour into a heavy pot or double boiler. Bring to a low boil and cook for 15 minutes.

Straining the Soymilk

Set a colander over a large bowl or pot and line the colander with a large piece (about 2 to 3 feet square) of nylon mesh or several layers of cheesecloth. Pour or ladle the cooked soybean mixture into the cloth-lined colander. Gather up two corners of the cloth in each hand and raise the ball of pulp a few inches out of the colander. Roll it back and forth in the cloth by alternately raising and lowering each hand. This will release most of the soymilk. Set the cloth and contents back into the colander, gather up the ends of the cloth again and twist them together until the cloth tightens around the ball of pulp.

Press the bundle with a wooden paddle or a jar to extract as much milk as possible. You can open the cloth up after you have pressed out all the milk, and mix 2 to 3 cups of boiling water into the pulp. Twist the cloth back up and press again. The pulp can be reserved for baking.

Some of the recipes in this book call for soymilk. When making tofu, you can reserve part of the soymilk to use in cooking later. Remember to adjust the amount of curding agent to maintain the correct proportions. Soymilk also makes a tasty, nutritious drink when sweetened, and can be served either hot or chilled.

Pressing the soymilk

Adding the curding agent to the soymilk

Finished curds and whey

Curding the Soymilk

Dilute ½ cup of vinegar in 1½ cups of hot water. For other curding agents see the table below. For the highest yield of tofu, the curding should be done slowly (in a few stages). This provides large, soft curds and yields a tofu high in water content.

Stir the freshly strained soymilk in a slow circular motion while it is still hot (about 185° F.). Stop the paddle upright to create a turbulence and immediately add 1¼ cups of the vinegar solution over the top of the soymilk, cover to retain the heat and let it sit undisturbed for 5 minutes. The soymilk will start to form large white curds. If there is still soymilk present, poke gently to activate curding and gently stir in the remaining ¼ cup vinegar solution. Cover the pot again and leave it 2 to 3 more minutes.

The curds are complete when they are surrounded by the clear yellow liquid called *whey*. If a very firm tofu is desired, the curds in the whey may be placed back on the heat and boiled a few minutes.

If there is a lot of whey and only a few curds, the beans may not have been ground finely enough, resulting in thin milk and low yield.

The whey acts as a natural detergent and will suds easily if stirred. It is good for washing and soaking the pots and cloths used during the tofu-making process.

Now the curds are ready to be pressed.

CURDING AGENTS

Soybeans	Warm Water	Curding Agent
1 lb. (2 1/2 cups)	1 cup	1/4 cup vinegar or lemon juice
1 lb. (2 1/2 cups)	1 1/2 cups	1 1/2 to 2 tsp. Nigari or Epsom salts
2 lbs. (5 cups)	1 1/2 cups	1/2 cup vinegar or lemon juice
2 lbs. (5 cups)	2 cups	3 to 4 tsp. Nigari or Epsom salts

Dipping out the whey

Ladling the curds into a cloth-lined colander

Pressing the Tofu

Line your colander or pressing box with a nylon mesh cloth or several layers of cheesecloth and set it up in the sink or over a bowl or pot.

Set the pot of curds and whey next to it. Set a large strainer in the pot to fill with whey, but keep the curds out. Then ladle out whey until most of it is out of the pot. This will help the curds form together into a nice solid tofu.

Next, ladle the curds into the colander or pressing box lined with the cloth.

Fold the cloth tightly around the curds, top with a flat plate and a weight. A half-gallon or gallon jar filled with water makes a good weight, or you can use a clean, heavy rock or brick. Press for 20 to 30 minutes. For firmer tofu use a heavier weight or press for a longer time.

When you remove the weight and the plate and fold back the cloth, the tofu should be firm to the touch. Gently remove the block of tofu from the colander or pressing box, and set it in a sink or bowl of cold water. Remove the cloth and leave the block in the water until it is cool and firm.

Store your tofu in a container of cold water in the refrigerator, changing the water daily to preserve freshness. It will keep this way up to one week.

Care and Maintenance of Equipment

Clean your milk-making equipment and cloth well immediately after each use. A mild soap solution may be used. Cloths can be soaked in bleach water occasionally after washing. A vegetable brush is a good cleaning tool for your colander, press and cloth. For easiest cleaning, soak the pot used for cooking the soymilk in water immediately after emptying. You will probably have to use a copper or stainless steel scrubber on that pot. Keep everything clean as you make your soymilk and tofu. The sooner your utensils are washed or rinsed, the easier they are to clean.

INDEX